LEADERSHIP
Unveiled

ELEVATING LEADERSHIP THROUGH EXPERIENCE

AN ANTHOLOGY

Visionary and Lead Author
Angela Hooper-Menifield,
MPA, SPHR, SCP

www.TrueVinePublishing.org

Leadership Unveiled: An Anthology
Angela Hooper-Menifield

Published by True Vine Publishing
810 Dominican Dr
Nashville, Tennessee
www.truevinepublishing.org

ISBN: 978-1-968092-16-0 Paperback
ISBN: 978-1-968092-17-7 eBook

Scripture quotations marked KJV are taken from the Holy Bible, King James Version.

Scripture taken from THE MESSAGE. Copyright © 1993, 1994, 1995, 1996, 2000, 2001, 2002. Used by permission of NavPress Publishing Group.

Scripture quotations taken from The Holy Bible, New International Version® NIV® Copyright © 1973, 1978, 1984, 2011 by Biblica, Inc. Used with permission. All rights reserved worldwide.

Scripture quotations taken from the (NASB®) New American Standard Bible®, Copyright © 1960, 1971, 1977, 1995, 2020 by The Lockman Foundation. Used by permission. All rights reserved. lockman.org

Scripture quotations marked TPT are from The Passion Translation®. Copyright © 2017, 2018, 2020 by Passion & Fire Ministries, Inc. Used by permission. All rights reserved. ThePassionTranslation.com.

Printed in the United States of America–First Edition

The views and opinions expressed in each chapter are those of the respective authors and do not necessarily reflect the views of the editor or the publisher.

A Note from the Visionary

*W*hen I envisioned *Leadership Unveiled*, I wasn't interested in producing just another book filled with leadership theories, frameworks, or high-profile names. I wanted to bring together real voices: diverse, dynamic, and deeply experienced individuals who are living leadership every day. I envisioned a collection that would both affirm what we know and challenge our assumptions about what it truly means to lead.

Leadership isn't a title. It isn't tenure. Leadership is a choice, a daily commitment to rise, to serve, to stretch, and to make space for others to do the same. This anthology was born from that belief. Within these pages, you'll find stories of transformation, hard-earned wisdom, practical strategies, and powerful insights from 12 remarkable leaders. Together, we've pulled back the curtain, unveiling leadership as it is: human, messy, intentional, and deeply impactful when done well.

Each author featured here was hand-selected, not solely for their professional accolades, but for their passion for growth, their dedication to developing others, and their authentic commitment to leading with purpose. They didn't show up to impress. They came to invest.

They wrote with courage and clarity, drawing on their lived experiences, whether in corporate boardrooms, nonprofit organizations, classrooms, entrepreneurial ventures, or at home with their families. We span generations, industries, and backgrounds, yet we are united by a shared mission: to leave leadership better than we found it.

I hope you won't just read this book, but that you'll reflect, apply, and shift. Let these pages mentor you. Let them stir something within you. Let them remind you that your leadership matters.

If you're ready to go deeper, we invite you to join us beyond the book. This anthology is only the beginning. Masterminds, workshops, and coaching experiences await those ready to become the kind of leader others choose to follow.

On behalf of all the authors, thank you for trusting us with your time, your attention, and your growth. Here's to leadership that is unmasked, unfiltered, and unapologetically real.

With purpose and power,
Angela Hooper-Menifield, MPA, SPHR, SCP
Visionary & Lead Author

TABLE OF *Contents*

I

The Foundations
of
Leadership

*B*efore anyone follows your lead, they meet your mindset, values, and presence. Leadership doesn't begin with a title or a team; it starts in the quiet choices, inner clarity, and personal growth that shape how you show up.

In this section, you'll uncover your authentic leadership identity, strengthen the mindset to thrive, and master tools like emotional intelligence and influence. Whether you lead in a boardroom, a classroom, or your community, these principles rise above roles and titles.

Leadership begins here, within you. Let's get to work.

CHAPTER 1

THE LEADER WITHIN:
UNVEILING YOUR AUTHENTIC LEADERSHIP IDENTITY

Dr. Cheryl Burton

*M*ost people think of a leader as someone appointed, promoted, or elected. While those are common paths, I want you to see yourself as a leader, starting now. Leadership begins with choosing yourself first. It's about how you lead your life, the relationships you build, and the influence you have. Your leadership style is one of the greatest predictors of how you will perform in any other leadership role.

In this chapter, I'll share a concept that has helped me navigate life's challenges and transitions while reaching personal and professional goals: the gift of "self-leadership." There's power in shaping and developing your identity as a leader. Our greatest asset is the ability to think and make decisions that serve both our best interests and the good of others.

Your life is not just about you. What are you modeling? What legacy will you leave behind? Every day, you are becoming a certain kind of leader either by default or by design. You can leave it to chance, hoping things work out, or you can be intentional, defining who you want to be and the life you want to lead.

Effective self-leadership involves the following critical components:

1. Self-Awareness: Understanding your strengths, weaknesses, values, and motivations. You cannot lead your life by design without awareness of who you are.
2. Goal Setting: The ability to establish clear, achievable objectives to guide your personal and professional development. Living your life by design requires discipline to achieve your goals, which is the ability to give yourself a command and follow through with it.
3. Self-Regulation- The ability to manage your emotions, to be intentional, and to remain focused and productive.
4. Self-Motivation- The ability to cultivate intrinsic drive, take initiative, and persevere through challenges. Let challenges be your propellers, not your deflators—choose to be propelled by purpose.
5. Self-Reflection- The ability to regularly assess your progress and learn from experience to improve future -performance. Be open to self-scrutiny, and self-exploration, no matter how difficult or uncomfortable.

Navigating the Path to Self-Leadership

As children, we were told what to do, how to behave, and we obeyed out of respect or fear. Sometimes we were given an explanation, the "why," which was always important to me, even if it meant frustrating my disciplinarian father. There were certain expectations of us as children, and we complied to make our parents and elders proud, or to evade punishment. Good behavior was rewarded, and for the most part, that is what shaped me.

Despite this child-rearing approach, we were always encouraged to do our best, and there was no question that we were loved and supported. However, there was also a part of me that was very curious, inquisitive, and not so willing to acquiesce to a demand or request, just because it was stated.

I remember how it felt as a child, the third of six surviving children, when I was told what to do, or not do, often without explanation, except that it was the "proper" thing to do. So, I grew up with this penchant for asking questions, wanting to know the reasons why. I guess that was the early indication of who I would become professionally and as a person. I would lead with questions.

Over the years, it became apparent that I was able to influence others and had become a reliable resource to my family members, friends, colleagues, and clients. This was aided by my interest in listening and observing to understand what was being communicated both verbally and non-verbally. I had a very strong desire to be heard and understood; if I felt that way, I assumed that other people had the same desire.

Although I was not familiar with the term "self-leadership" in my youth, in retrospect, that is what I was developing. I have since learned that to be more intentional in my self-leadership development is an indispensable part of my continuous growth.

The following are self-leadership lessons I've embraced and implemented as I continue to develop and unveil my authentic leadership identity:

1. There Is A Force Greater Than Me That I Can Always Turn to for Guidance.

I am never alone. All I must do is be still and look inward. I know I was created fully equipped and well-resourced to live a life of purpose and become who I am meant to be. This truth has given me the confidence to navigate unfamiliar and uncomfortable spaces, knowing I am connected to a greater power and am part of a much larger life system. Spiritual connection is my lifeline.

2. Mindset is essential to our growth.

As James Allen, the well-known author, states: "As a man thinketh, so is he". Everything begins with how we think. Embracing this truth led me to start "Thinking Tuesday," a Facebook Live series sharing how we can control our thoughts and shape the results they produce. We have adopted the slogan for Thinking Tuesday, "Your Mind is a Garden; Your thoughts are the seeds; You can grow flowers, or you can grow weeds". In essence, you are the gardener who plants and cultivates your thoughts, good or bad. James Allen also states something similar: "Man's mind may be likened to a garden, which may be intelligently cultivated or allowed to run wild."

> **"EVERYTHING BEGINS WITH HOW WE THINK."**

This statement is so empowering because it reinforces the resources that we each have within us, many we are unaware of.

Why Not Learn How to Program Your Brain to Default to Positive Thoughts?

My continuous journey into self-discovery, self-leadership, and enhancing my services has led me to obtain additional certifications beyond my academic degrees. One of which is a Neuroencoding Specialist. I am a One-Star Dual Elite Neuroencoding Specialist, trained by Joseph McClendon, III, a renowned neuropsychologist and founder of the Neuroencoding Institute.

Through this certification, I've been trained in the Neuroencoding Methodology, a powerful approach that helps my clients achieve results faster and reach further than they ever imagined possible. I guide them in developing a strong self-leadership identity by teaching them how to actively engage their brain in targeted ways that interrupt unhelpful thoughts, emotions, and behavior patterns. Together, we replace these with intentional, empowering thoughts and actions that, over time, become their natural, default response in challenging situations.

> "AS I THINK, SO I FEEL. AS I FEEL, SO I DO. AS I DO, I HAVE A RESULT."

These methods reduce or eliminate complexity by simplifying their understanding of how we all function: "As I think, so I feel. As I feel, so I do. As I do, I have a result." This simple formula helps in the development of the leader within and the understanding of the role we play in the results we achieve when leading with intention and purpose. We will always get a result, and we can be instrumental in determining what that result will be by deciding what and how we think (e.g., abundance or scarcity, fear or courage, positive or negative).

Taking a retrospective look at my leadership journey, I recall my post-graduate training as a psychotherapist at Washington Square Institute for Psychotherapy and Mental Health in New York City. A key requirement was entering individual therapy with an institutionally trained therapist to experience the method first-hand, explore my personal development, and learn to manage transference, countertransference, and other therapeutic issues.

Now, I train as a Neuroencoding Specialist, and I find myself confronted by a similar experience. Said more directly: "Physician, Heal Thyself". This mantra reminds me that I must use the same methods to help me navigate life that I use with my clients. In other words, I can't simply teach theory. I must experience it for myself.

This further promotes the development and unveiling of the leader within. I am utilizing the same neuroencoding techniques on myself as I teach my clients (e.g., STOP technique to manage anxiety, procrastination, overwhelm, self-doubt, fear of failure, fear of success, Imposter Syndrome, etc. The Mirror Exercise to celebrate accomplishments, build self-confidence, etc.). These techniques directly engage the brain and are reinforced by physical activities.

3. The Peace You Seek is Already within You.

Yes, it is that simple, but it is often very elusive. We tend to seek answers outside of ourselves, and as a result, end up frustrated, dissatisfied, angry, feeling defeated, depressed, and a host of other negative feelings that really can be avoided.

I am not making light of this reality; it can be difficult to look within ourselves. Self-scrutiny can be painful because we often find aspects of ourselves that we don't want to see, things we don't want to admit about ourselves. We avoid seeing and owning our bad habits because we are then confronted with having to change, and change is not easy. This avoidance contributes to the elusiveness of the peace that we seek.

Famous author, Donald Walsh, puts it like this: "If you don't go within, you will go without." Developing the leader within requires an inward journey, not sometimes, but all the time. Self-assessment is indispensable if you are to be authentic, allowing your vulnerabilities to be exposed and holding yourself accountable.

> "DEVELOPING THE LEADER WITHIN REQUIRES AN INWARD JOURNEY."

I recently experienced a breakthrough when I recognized the reason behind my frustration with someone's actions. It was there before me all along, but I was not ready nor willing to accept it. The change began as I changed my perspective on that experience.

You cannot imagine the relief I felt when I released my expectations and confronted what I had to do within myself to make the change occur. The peace I was seeking outside of myself was already within me. I had to own it. I had to embrace it and let go of the thinking that was leading to my frustration and disappointment, and move forward, knowing that I have control of how I think, and how that would affect my feelings, and then my actions.

The challenge that most people have is that we want to see changes in our environment and relationships without making changes within ourselves. To grow in this area, my inner leader had to rely on one of my favorite guiding quotes:

"When you change the way you look at things, the things you look at change." –Wayne Dyer

This brief statement has carried me a long way, and I've come to truly appreciate it as a game-changer. When we hold on to a perspective for dear life, refuse to make a shift, however small, we miss opportunities to grow beyond our comfort zone and discover how magnificent we truly are.

4. Embrace the Pain of Growth.

Breaking News: There is no growth without pain. That's the truth. The developing leader within will encounter many challenges that may have you question whether you can surmount them, or if the challenge is worth it. What keeps me going is monitoring my thoughts. Doing a cerebral checkup to see where I might need to adjust my thinking or how my thoughts are serving me.

I often try to understand my growth using the metaphor of working out or exercising. When returning to the gym after being absent for a while, my muscles ache so badly that I am more focused on the pain than the gain. However, if I can understand the purpose of the pain, I find I will embrace it because it is signaling that my muscles are being stretched, and that I need to continue exercising to be able to see and experience the gains. Ultimately, my muscles strengthen, the pain lessens, and there is more comfort in my movements. In fact, I find that I can stretch deeper, reach for higher goals, and celebrate breaking barriers that were previously self-limiting. Such is growth.

Self-leadership requires the ability to coach ourselves through difficult decisions and against compromises that will keep us from unveiling our true leadership identity and limiting our potential. As I write this chapter, I am facing one of the biggest challenges one could face: the care of my 103-year-old mother. Previously very independent, my mother has experienced a significant decline in her health in a few short months. While grateful for the full life lived, this season still comes with its challenges.

Personal Reflection

I find this season of life to be a very humbling experience. It has reminded me that even with my strengths as an advocate, coordinator, and encourager, I can still feel vulnerable when the path forward is uncertain. It has taught me the value of seeking the expertise of others who are better qualified to attend to her needs.

The true leader within has to know when to delegate, hire out or even take a backseat. So often we view leadership as being in the forefront. This season has been a reminder that such is not always the case. In addition, the issue of prioritization has also been key to this experience of self-leadership.

So often, everything appears to occupy the same

level of importance, yet everything cannot be managed at the same level of importance. I've learned to delegate to others those duties and issues that do not need my direct intervention, and to trust the ability of those to whom I delegate, to mitigate unnecessary anxiety and overwhelm.

Self-Care

"You can't give what you don't have" is a mantra that keeps me watchful of my self-care, which includes attending to my physical, emotional, and spiritual needs. Journaling, meditation, and devotional readings assist in processing my thoughts and feelings.

Self-Compassion

Setting realistic expectations for myself has allowed me to accept my limitations, develop an attitude of gratitude, and accept that every day will not be perfect.

Final Thoughts

I hope that this chapter inspires you as you continue to develop and unveil your authentic leadership identity. May you be encouraged to keep growing and to do the unavoidable and indispensable inner work to live by design and not by default.

As I conclude this chapter on unveiling authentic leadership, I find it essential to dedicate these reflections to my mother, who recently passed away. Her unwavering spirit profoundly shaped my understanding of self-leadership. Throughout our journey together, especially during the challenging times of her illness, I discovered invaluable lessons about resilience, self-acceptance, and the true meaning of leadership.

My mother exemplified perseverance and patience—two qualities I now recognize as essential components of authentic leadership. Despite enduring months of pain, she approached each day with grace, never wavering in her faith and hope. Her ability to remain cooperative and positive in the face of adversity taught me the power of cultivating a resilient mindset, not only in leadership, but in life itself.

In her quiet strength, I found lessons in self-assessment and the courage to embrace the pain that often accompanies growth. Caring for her reinforced the truth that to lead others effectively, we must first care for ourselves. I learned to delegate, to honor my limitations, and to reach out for support. These are lessons I will carry forward in both life and leadership.

As I reflect on our shared experience, I am filled with gratitude for her enduring patience and unwavering positivity. She was always looking for the silver lining, even in the darkest moments. My mother's legacy is one of love, strength, and hope. It is with deep appreciation that I dedicate this chapter to her.

May her spirit inspire all who seek to unveil their authentic leadership identity, reminding us that true leadership is rooted in the virtues of perseverance and patience.

CHAPTER 2

WHY MINDSET MATTERS

Leslie Britt

"Point your kids in the right direction, when they're old, they won't be lost."

— Proverbs 22:6 (MSG)

"Leadership is influence, nothing more, nothing less."

— John Maxwell

Leadership Begins at Home

I was the youngest of 13 children, eight girls and five boys. My father, a World War II Marine Corps veteran, was our living, breathing example of leadership in action. He did not just lead our large family; he led himself with discipline, integrity, and purpose. Alongside my mother, his life partner and co-leader, they raised us with timeless values: respect, love, and gratitude.

I remember watching a tribute to Barbara Walters shortly after her passing. During the special, I noticed something subtle but powerful. When she asked those being interviewed about their mothers, their responses were kind, thoughtful, and warm. When she asked about their fathers, the responses were quite different. They were either tears of joy or tears of pain, no middle ground.

That contrast caused me to reflect: there is something "uniquely connected" to the role of a father. When fathers are present in the lives of their children, modeling leadership and values, they become powerful influences, shaping identity, offering guidance, and providing emotional security. In many ways, fathers represent how to lead, how to show up, and how to love. Their presence can bring tears of joy, as children feel seen, supported, and deeply loved. However, when a child's experience of their father is marked by absence, neglect, or harmful behavior, fathers can also become the source of tears of pain. They leave wounds where there should have been warmth, confusion where there should have been clarity, and longing where there should have been love.

> **"FATHERS REPRESENT HOW TO LEAD, HOW TO SHOW UP, AND HOW TO LOVE."**

That night, something stirred in me. It reminded me of the legacy my father left behind, and how his mindset formed the foundation of the leader, man, and father I am today. As an executive coach, I often return to one unshakable truth: mindset matters most. Who you are begins with how you think about yourself, about others, and about what is possible. It's not just about your skill set or your résumé; it's about how you lead your life. True leadership always starts on the inside.

"Listen to my correction, my sons, for I speak to you as your father. Let discernment enter your heart, and you will grow wise with the understanding I impart." (Proverbs 4:1-2, TPT).

I did not realize I was learning about leadership as a child, but evidently, I was, every day. I was learning through watching my dad lead with quiet strength, through seeing how he treated others, and through observing how he responded to life's ups and downs. His relationship with God shaped his actions. His mindset shaped his influence.

I grew up playing basketball and football with some guys who did not have fathers. I recall the times we all played in our backyard. If foul language was used, my dad would correct the person, noting that it should not be used, and explaining why. It was obvious that my dad left an indelible impression on many of the guys from my neighborhood, even some who may have taken the wrong path in life. After returning home from several years of military service, I met many people who asked about my dad and still recalled the lessons he taught them. Those lessons were planted not only in my heart but in theirs as well, by a man they saw as a steady and consistent presence.

When I returned home from military service, the bond between my dad and me grew even deeper. During those years, I saw him not just as my dad, but as a man of character, purpose, and unwavering faith. What he taught me then is what I teach now. These are more than life lessons. They are mindset markers. They shape how we think, how we lead, and how we live.

The Mindset Lessons My Father Taught Me

Respect Everyone, Including Yourself
"Be devoted to one another in brotherly love; give preference to one another in honor" (Romans 12:10, NASB).

Respect is not just about manners; it is about mindset. My father taught us to honor others, no matter their background, appearance, or social status. He never allowed us to treat anyone as less than human, and he modeled that conviction in how he spoke to strangers, how he handled conflict, and how he served our community. Even more foundational than respect for others was the idea of self-respect. He taught us that you must believe in your value before you can truly see the value in others.

> **"RESPECT IS NOT JUST ABOUT MANNERS; IT IS ABOUT MINDSET."**

That truth took root in me early and shaped how I moved through the world. Self-respect builds a mindset of quiet confidence strong enough to stand tall, yet humble enough to listen. It teaches you how to walk into any room, from the corner store to a corporate boardroom, with your head held high, not because of ego, but because you know who you are. Just as important, it teaches you how to extend that same dignity to others, even when they're different, difficult, or down on their luck.

My father showed us how to meet people where they are, but never shrink from who you are to do it. That balance between authenticity and adaptability has been my compass. It guided me through the disciplined structure of military service, through conversations in foreign lands, and back to my neighborhood with the same steady sense of identity. Whether speaking to leaders or listening to those often overlooked, I've carried that mindset like a well-worn tool: respect, rooted in self-respect, shaping how I see others and how I carry myself.

Give Your Best Every Time

"Put your heart and soul into everything you do, as though you are doing it for the Lord himself and not merely for others" (Colossians 3:23, TPT).

Being early was not a suggestion; it was a standard. Being on time meant being late. Showing up ready meant you honored the work. Whatever job I had, I was taught to give it my all.

Mindset matters here as well: your effort reflects your belief in your purpose. People who believe in what they are doing do not settle for mediocrity. They go the extra mile, not for applause, but because excellence is who they are. Excellence is not about applause; it is about purpose-driven honor.

This mindset will separate you from the crowd and allow you to excel in the opportunities that come your way.

Do Not Cut Corners

"Enter through the narrow gate..." (Matthew 7:13, NIV).

I will never forget one afternoon, while I was walking home from elementary school. My dad watched me jaywalk on the way home. I arrived at the first step leading to the front door when he calmly instructed me to walk back and cross the street the right way at the stop sign, using the crosswalk.

"Don't cut corners in life," he said.

That moment has been etched in my mind, and his voice echoes through every major decision I've made. At the time, it felt like a small thing, but over time, I realized it wasn't about the street. It was about the habit.

Cutting corners may seem quick, but it costs more than you think. You may save time in the moment, but you compromise integrity, miss valuable lessons, or set patterns that can lead to bigger mistakes down the road.

Doing things the right way, no matter how small, builds discipline, attention to detail, and a mindset of excellence. My father was teaching me that how I do anything is how I'll do everything. That one walk back to the crosswalk turned into a life of walking with purpose, principle, and without apology.

After my time in boot camp, while out on liberty in downtown San Diego with other sailors, I watched a group of guys run through traffic to get to the other side of the street without properly crossing at the light. They were met by a police officer who delivered a stern lecture about the dangers of crossing the street against traffic. Immediately, my mind shifted back to my dad's words of wisdom: "Do not cut corners in life."A disciplined mindset sees the long game and chooses the harder right over the easier wrong.

Be a Lifelong Learner
"Education is the passport to the future, for tomorrow belongs to those who prepare for it today."

– Malcolm X.

Learning never stops. Mindset shapes your growth trajectory, whether you see failure as a defeat or as a doorway. In the Navy, mentors outside my direct chain of command took me under their wings. Their investment in me changed my life. I kept my mind open and my spirit willing to learn, and that mindset has served me in rooms with world leaders and neighborhood youth alike.

I have disciplined myself to continue to learn, remain curious, ask questions, and seek growth in every area of my life. This mindset will guide me for as long as I have breath in my body.

Integrity Matters

"Integrity is doing the right thing, even when no one is watching." –C.S. Lewis.

My dad valued truth over lies, regardless of the situation or the outcome. Being truthful at all times is an indication of your integrity. Having a "mindset for integrity" is especially important and needed in the world today. Integrity is what holds everything else together: your reputation, your relationships, and your ability to lead.

"MINDSET SHAPES YOUR GROWTH TRAJECTORY."

Without it, talent is wasted, trust is broken, and success becomes shallow. In a world that often rewards shortcuts, spin, and self-interest, integrity sets you apart. It's not always easy, and it's not always popular, but it is always right.

My father taught us that who you are when no one is watching is who you are, and if you compromise the truth in small things, it becomes easier to compromise in big things. Integrity builds credibility, and credibility opens doors that only character can keep open. It's not just about being honest; it's about being whole.

The Gift I Never Asked For

In October 2023, I was provided a form to fill out for a program, and one of the questions was: "What is the greatest gift you've ever received?"

My first thoughts were about my child's birth and my faith journey. Then I remembered the day I drove my dad to the Marine Corps Ball. He was 97 years old. During the drive to that time-honored ceremony where the youngest and oldest Marines cut the cake together, my dad turned to me and said something I will never forget.

He said, "I love you, and I'm proud of the man you've become."

That was it. That was the gift.

It wasn't wrapped or planned. It was earned through years of shared values, mutual respect, and a mindset of love and leadership.

Why It Matters Today

The mindset my father exhibited, shaped by his faith in God, left a legacy. He did not have a manual on how to be a great dad, but he had the Word, and that was enough. His mindset formed the roots of the man I am today.

These lessons have carried me through military service, into marriage, into fatherhood, across cultures, and into my coaching practice. Now, I intentionally pass them to my son, not just through what I say, but through the way I live.

I will model integrity, faith, courage, and curiosity.

I will teach him to lead with wisdom and walk in purpose.

I will guide him to ask big questions, live with a grateful heart, and serve others well.

Call to Action

Now, I ask you: What mindset are you passing on? What lessons will echo after your time on this earth has passed? Let today be the day you choose a higher standard. Lead with love. Live with purpose. Let your mindset be your message.

> **"YOUR LEGACY WILL NOT JUST BE WHAT YOU ACCOMPLISHED BUT WHO YOU RAISED...INFLUENCED AND ...BECAME"**

Your legacy will not just be what you accomplished but who you raised, who you influenced, and who you became. The world does not just need more leaders; the world needs more leaders with the right mindset. Will you be one of them?

CHAPTER 3

LEADING WITH EMOTIONAL INTELLIGENCE:

THE UNSEEN ADVANTAGE

Dr. Robin K. Butler

*Y*ou lost your temper.

You were awake, worrying half the night.

You couldn't get past what happened last week, or even yesterday.

Whatever the case, we've all been there: lost and under the control of a mirage of feelings we'd rather not experience. Logically, we get it; we're in the wrong headspace, but how do we manage to take back control from the emotions that hold us hostage?

It might help to consider each of these emotions as though they were a person. Think *Snow White and the Seven Dwarfs*. Many of us remember that these guys were more like bullies in high school. You know, the kids who caused mayhem every time they showed up. Let's take a minute to get to know their names:

- Anger
- Fear
- Shame
- Anxiety
- Apathy
- Despair
- Guilt

Whew, tough crowd, right? But don't be intimidated. First of all, don't forget that all emotions serve a purpose. Even these.

In one moment, I experienced happiness, and then suddenly, sadness. Like me, you may experience a barrage of emotions; perhaps you feel a hundred different things in a single day, but how do you manage them? This question might not be quite as easy to answer as you think.

Of course, these emotions are never quite so simple, are they? It's when they get out of control that they become trouble. There's no easy, one-size-fits-all definition of emotions, but we're going to focus on leading with emotional intelligence and how you have the unseen advantage when you understand your emotions and how they can serve you well.

So, no more roller coasters. No more nightmares. No more self-sabotage. Emotional mastery is around the corner. Let's dive in.

Let's Get Emotional...

In today's ever-evolving business world, emotional intelligence (EI) isn't simply a buzzword; it's an often-overlooked asset in the world of leadership, and it's time for it to be unveiled. While technical and business acumen are essential, the unseen advantage of emotional intelligence can elevate a leader's effectiveness.

In the realm of leadership, emotional intelligence is a differentiator; it's the secret weapon that can redefine success. While many leaders focus on and chase technical skills, the true game-changer lies in mastering the invisible force of emotional intelligence. Those who attain emotional mastery truly hold the unseen advantage, both personally and professionally, among their colleagues.

What Is Emotional Intelligence All About?

Daniel Goleman is widely recognized as the father of emotional intelligence. His research led to the foundational efforts in assessing emotional quotient (EQ) alongside intelligence quotient (IQ). Emotional intelligence encompasses four core components: self-awareness, self-management, social awareness, and relationship management.

Mastering these facets can help leaders navigate the complexities of human interactions and foster a positive organizational environment. By embracing emotional intelligence, leaders can influence their teams in ways that traditional skills cannot.

It's important to note that managing our emotions intelligently creates harmony in all areas of our lives.

The Framework

Self-Awareness: The Foundation

Self-awareness is the cornerstone of emotional intelligence. It is the foundation of effective leadership. It refers to the ability to recognize and comprehend your emotions, strengths, opportunities, influence, and the impact you have on others.

For leaders, this insight is critical. Leaders who possess self-awareness can assess how their feelings affect their behavior and decision-making. This understanding allows them to stay grounded during challenging situations and establishes a sense of authenticity with which team members often resonate. Instead of reacting negatively when facing obstacles, self-aware leaders can reflect on their emotions and respond thoughtfully. This reflection cultivates a culture of openness, where team members feel safe to express their own emotions and ideas.

I've adopted a philosophy that "you must know yourself to grow yourself." It's the impetus of emotional intelligence. Think of it as planting seeds, watering them, and reaping a harvest; that's the foundation. You may not see the growth in the beginning, but eventually, you'll reap the harvest of self-awareness.

> **"YOU MUST KNOW YOURSELF TO GROW YOURSELF."**

My Tips for Cultivating Self-Awareness (REAP)

R - Reflect Daily: Spend a few minutes each day reflecting on your emotions. What went right or wrong? What triggered the feeling or emotion? How did you respond? Journaling can help track your emotional patterns over time.

E - Embrace Feedback: Never shy away from input. Receive it as a gift. Encourage family and team members to share their honest opinions about your leadership style. This can unveil blind spots and areas for growth.

A - Assess Your Behavior: Tools like the DISC or the Enneagram can provide valuable insights into your personality, communication, and leadership styles, highlighting strengths and opportunities for improvement.

P - Practice Mindfulness: Engage in mindfulness techniques, which can help you remain present and become more aware of your thoughts and feelings.

Self-Management: The Force

Once you grasp self-awareness, the next step is self-management. It's about mastery. It refers to the ability to regulate one's emotions and behaviors in countless situations. Leaders who practice self-management can calmly navigate conflicts and pressures, demonstrating resilience in the face of adversity.

Emotionally intelligent leaders are nimble and well-equipped to pivot and concentrate on constructive situations, rather than lose their footing by allowing frustration and anger to influence their actions. This ability not only enhances their emotional stability but also serves as a powerful paradigm for their teams. When leaders model self-management, they inspire their team members to embrace the same approach, fostering a workplace environment that thrives on emotional harmony.

When you are self-aware and manage yourself successfully, this is your opportunity to become a force to be reckoned with. Leaders often face high-stress circumstances and pressure; managing these emotions is crucial to leading efficiently. As the force, you must develop a plan to combine power and influence to positively impact those around you.

Tips for Effective Self-Management (PLAN)

P - Pause Before Responding: In tense situations, I invite you to take a moment to breathe and gauge your emotions before reacting. YES! I want you to rate your reaction. This can prevent knee-jerk responses that may further escalate the situation. Remember: "Peace, not pieces." We want to make peace, not leave things in pieces due to emotional reactions.

L - Leverage Resilience: Embrace challenges and setbacks as opportunities for growth. Learning to display grace under pressure and bounce back from adversity enhances both personal and team morale.

A - Adapt and Set Personal Goals: Align your emotional goals with your professional ones. For instance, if you struggle with patience, remind yourself to take a step back and give team members time to present their ideas. Make the necessary adjustments and tailor your plan to ensure it works for you and your team; no cookie-cutter approaches here.

N - Navigate and Implement Coping Strategies: Identify techniques that help you manage stress, whether it's exercise, deep breathing, or creative hobbies. Implement these strategies proactively rather than reactively. It's about your well-being, because we understand that mental and physical health are related.

Social Awareness: The Focus

The third component, social awareness, underscores the importance of empathizing with others' emotions and perspectives. This skill is critical for leaders because it fosters a supportive and collaborative culture within teams.

Socially aware leaders have a keen perception of the emotions of others, enabling them to navigate interpersonal dynamics effortlessly. They value being attuned to team members' feelings and can offer guidance and different perspectives when needed, fostering a sense of belonging within the organization.

These leaders focus and leverage their lens to anticipate potential challenges that may arise in team dynamics. Leaders can diffuse and often prevent conflict to maintain a harmonious work environment when they are focused and proactive. The vision of the socially aware leader is like the eagle: they focus as they soar, building trust and strengthening relationships that lead to enhanced collaboration and productivity.

Have you ever seen an eagle soar through the sky? It's majestic and has significant meaning. An eagle flying high gives us perspective on rising higher and getting beyond our limiting beliefs, and being able to focus and see things from a different point of view. I have always been fascinated by eagles and learned that they possess sharp vision that is significantly better than humans. This vision allows them to focus and spot their prey from afar. When we focus, we can become more socially aware.

Tips for Enhancing Social Awareness (SOAR)

S - Show Empathy: When engaging with team members, strive to understand their perspectives. Ask open-ended questions about their experiences and feelings to deepen your connection.

O - Observe Nonverbal Cues: Pay attention to body language and tone of voice. Often, these nonverbal signals reveal more than words alone.

A - Active Listening: Practice active listening by giving your full attention to the speaker. Confirm understanding by paraphrasing what was said and asking for clarification when needed.

R - Remember Inclusivity: Foster an environment where everyone feels comfortable sharing their thoughts. Encourage team members from different backgrounds to voice their opinions.

Relationship Management: The Formulation

Building Connections

The ability to navigate social complexities and manage relationships effectively is what differentiates great leaders. Relationship management is about leveraging your emotional intelligence to maintain and build strong relationships with team members.

The final pillar of emotional intelligence is relationship management. This encompasses the skills necessary to build, maintain, and repair relationships. Effective relationship management enables leaders to communicate openly, resolve conflicts, and inspire their teams.

Strong leaders understand that their ability to connect with others can significantly impact team morale and performance. By prioritizing positive interactions and fostering a culture of support, leaders can cultivate an environment where creativity and innovation flourish. When teams feel valued and understood, they are more likely to engage and contribute wholeheartedly to organizational goals.

Tips for Mastering Relationship Management (CALM)

C - Communicate Openly: Transparency is key. Share your thoughts and feelings honestly, and encourage your team to do the same. Regular check-ins help keep communication flowing.

A - Acknowledge and Celebrate Achievements: Recognize and celebrate both individual and team accomplishments. This fosters trust and motivates your team to strive for excellence.

L - Learn and Leverage Conflict Management Skills: Develop your ability to address and mediate conflicts. Approach such situations with a solutions-oriented mindset, focusing on common ground.

M - Master Mentorship: Invest time in mentoring emerging leaders. By sharing your insights and experiences, you can cultivate a stronger team bond and inspire the next generation of leaders.

My Emotional Intelligence Story

I had a choice to make. Let's go back to the beginning. Do you remember the statement about *Snow White and the Seven Dwarfs* as it relates to emotions?

As a leader, I often reached for my typical allies: anger, fear, shame, anxiety, apathy, despair, and guilt. On any given day and in any given moment, there I was, allowing them to control me. I made friends with my "bullies" and allowed them to become my "allies." Bad choice, right?

I've learned that the best experience is not just the experience itself, but the lived and evaluated experience. I choose to learn, live, and evaluate. I was an HR leader charged with taking my company through a reorganization that, unfortunately, included a layoff that also impacted me. I was introduced to the works of Daniel Goleman before this assignment.

That leadership team participated in an emotional intelligence workshop, and I'm grateful that we did. It was a self-fulfilling prophecy. At the time, I did not realize that sitting in the workshop would aid me in my upcoming task and be the very thing that would catapult me as a leader and educator in EQ work.

I wrote the foundation, the force, the focus, and the formulation; it was personal to me. I first had to deal with myself and apply my *REAP principle*. The experience of laying off 69 other people and then myself stretched me beyond my typical capacity. Through that nine-month transition, I learned how to develop my *PLAN* principle.

It was the muscle that I needed to endure every challenge that I would face. Daily, I reminded myself of the keen sight of the eagle and the alignment of focus, enabling me to *SOAR* and increase my social awareness.

I won't say that it was easy. I was even asked to keep everything confidential and remain the consummate professional. After 30 days, I could tell my team that they were safe, but it was time to get to work. It was like the storm before the calm. I had to quickly pivot because I didn't have time for woe-is-me moments or pity parties; I had people to take care of during a major organizational transformation.

My *CALM* principle guided me and allowed me to exhibit grace under pressure. Who would've ever thought that a layoff experience would yield a positive experience that I can honestly say stretched and grew me as a leader? I grasped onto eliminating the traditional emotional roller coaster and opting for emotional intelligence.

The Unseen Advantage

Leaders who embrace and cultivate emotional intelligence find they have an unseen advantage over their counterparts. This isn't just about being a "nice" leader; it's about creating an empowered, engaged workforce that drives innovation and productivity.

Here's the real kicker: when leaders prioritize emotional intelligence, they create a ripple effect throughout their organization. The benefits extend beyond individual performance; they enhance team cohesion, increase employee satisfaction, and ultimately lead to better business results.

A Call to Action

So, what's the next step for you as a leader? Here's a simple guide to start your journey toward leading with emotional intelligence: **(PRESS)**

P - Practice Daily: Integrate emotional intelligence practices into your daily routine, whether it's mindfulness, active listening, or celebrating team successes.

R - Reflect and Adapt: Regularly reflect on your progress and adjust your strategies as needed. Continuous learning is key.

E - Encourage a Culture of EI: Foster a learning environment where team members feel comfortable discussing emotional intelligence and are encouraged to develop these skills as well.

S - Self-Assess: Take a self-assessment to evaluate your current level of emotional intelligence.

S - Set Goals: Identify one or two areas you'd like to improve, whether it's self-management or social awareness, and set measurable goals.

By focusing on emotional intelligence, you empower not only yourself but those around you. Leaders who invest in emotional intelligence will find that the unseen advantage translates into tangible results, both for themselves and their organizations. Step into this realm with confidence, compassion, and a commitment to growth. Lead with emotional intelligence, and watch how your leadership transforms.

Incorporating emotional intelligence into leadership practices offers a pathway to pivot from negative emotions to positive outcomes. It can be tempting for leaders to react impulsively, especially in high-pressure situations. However, by practicing self-awareness and self-management, leaders can choose to respond with empathy and constructive solutions rather than frustration or anger. This shift in approach not only enhances their leadership effectiveness but also empowers their teams. When leaders model emotional intelligence, they lay the groundwork for a culture of collaboration and support.

Emotional intelligence is not just essential for personal growth as a leader; it is a crucial component of business savvy. The rapidly changing business landscape often presents unforeseen challenges that require adaptability and emotional resilience. Leaders who hone their emotional intelligence are better equipped to handle stress, navigate organizational change, and foster resilience among their teams. In this way, emotional intelligence becomes a powerful tool to drive performance and maintain a competitive edge, setting emotionally intelligent leaders apart in today's workforce.

Ultimately, adopting emotional intelligence as a core leadership competency transforms not just the leader but the entire organization. By mastering self-awareness, self -management, social awareness, and relationship management, leaders can positively influence their teams, fostering an environment of trust and accountability.

The ripple effects of such emotional savvy can lead to increased employee engagement, improved team dynamics, and even higher overall performance. As the dynamics of work evolve, the need for emotionally intelligent leaders becomes more critical, emphasizing that success extends well beyond skills and education; it fundamentally relies on the power of positive emotions and authentic connections.

CHAPTER 4

THE INTERPLAY OF INFLUENCE, AUTHORITY, AND POWER

Kenric Lynn

*W*hen we think about power, what images come to mind? For many, it's the image of a leader at the head of a table, a general on the battlefield, or a CEO making decisions that ripple through an entire organization, but beneath the surface of these visible displays of power are two often misunderstood forces: influence and authority. These are the levers that move people, shape organizations, and even change the course of history.

During my years in the Army, I saw firsthand how influence and authority were both tested and wielded. From the very first day, the hierarchy was clear, not just in rank, but in the subtle ways people sought what I came to call the "final say-so." It wasn't just about who wore more stripes or stars. Sometimes, it was about who had the ear of the person in charge, or who could sway a room with a word or a look. The pursuit of the "final say-so" was constant, and it became clear that power was not just about position, but about the ability to shape outcomes.

One of my supervisors once told me, "Rank means nothing unless you have the final say-so." That phrase echoed in my mind throughout my career. As I advanced, I saw why people fought so hard for promotion. Sure, there were obvious benefits, better pay, more responsibility, but there was also the allure of greater power, authority, and, perhaps most importantly, influence.

But power is not always as straightforward as it seems. Sometimes, it's wielded by those who have no formal authority at all. I recall the installation commander's spouse who, despite holding no official rank, acted as if they did. Their influence was such that few dared to challenge them, fearing

"POWER IS NOT ALWAYS AS STRAIGHTFORWARD AS IT SEEMS. SOMETIMES, IT'S WIELDED BY THOSE WHO HAVE NO FORMAL AUTHORITY AT ALL."

the repercussions that might roll downhill if word reached the commander. Here was a perfect example of influence trumping authority: a person with no formal power, yet able to shape behavior and outcomes.

Contrast this with my experience at the Primary Leadership Development Course (PLDC), where newly promoted or soon-to-be-promoted soldiers took turns as squad leaders. Each of us was given authority over a small group, but only those who could earn the trust and respect of their peers truly wielded power. One squad leader, despite having formal authority, lost influence by making changes for personal benefit. Their authority was undermined by a lack of influence, leaving them isolated and ineffective.

This chapter explores the dynamic interplay between influence, authority, and power. We'll examine what it means to have power, how influence operates, where authority comes from, and how these forces combine to drive action and change. Along the way, we'll draw on research and real-world examples to illuminate the profound impact these forces have in every sphere of life.

Defining the Terms: Influence, Authority, and Power

Before we dive deeper, let's clarify our terms. As Mortimer J. Adler and Charles Van Doren suggest in their classic *How to Read a Book, understanding key terms is essential to understanding the argument.*

- Influence is the power to affect or change someone or something without directly forcing them. It's about shaping outcomes through persuasion, example, or relationships (Britannica, n.d.).
- Authority is the power or right to give orders, make decisions, and enforce obedience. It's typically tied to a formal position or recognized expertise (Britannica, n.d.).
- Power is the broader ability or right to control people or things. It can be derived from influence, authority, or both (Britannica, n.d.).

The Nature of Power

"Power tends to corrupt, and absolute power corrupts absolutely. Great men are almost always bad men, even when they exercise influence and not authority; still more when you superadd the tendency of the certainty of corruption by authority" (Lord Acton, letter to Bishop Mandell Creighton, 1887).

Power is a double-edged sword. It can be used to build or destroy, to help or to harm. As Lord Acton famously warned, power must be tamed and exercised responsibly. Research supports this caution: Dacher Keltner, a psychologist at UC Berkeley, found that people in positions of power are more likely to act impulsively, ignore social norms, and show less empathy (Keltner, 2016). Yet power can also amplify positive traits, generosity, vision, and courage, when wielded by those with strong values and self-awareness.

"POWER IS A DOUBLE-EDGED SWORD. IT CAN BE USED TO BUILD OR DESTROY, TO HELP OR TO HARM."

Consider the story of *He-Man and the Power Sword*. When Prince Adam raised his sword and declared, "I have the power!" he was transformed, but his core values remained. The sword amplified what was already inside him. In the real world, power works much the same way. It magnifies our values, principles, and morals. If we are generous, power enables us to give more. If we are short-tempered, power can make us tyrannical.

This is why self-knowledge is so critical. Research by David McClelland (1975) on the "need for power" found that individuals with a high need for power but low self-control are more likely to misuse authority. Conversely, those with high self-control use power to achieve positive outcomes for others.

Before seeking power, it's wise to reflect on our values and tendencies. Are we prepared to wield power responsibly? Do we understand the impact our actions can have on others? These questions are not just philosophical; they are practical, as the consequences of misused power can be profound.

Influence: The Hidden Force

John C. Maxwell, a renowned leadership expert, defines leadership simply as "influence, nothing more, nothing less." This may sound simplistic, but research supports Maxwell's assertion. In a classic study, French and Raven (1959) identified five bases of social power: legitimate, reward, coercive, expert, and referent. Of these, expert and referent power, both forms of influence, are often the most effective in driving lasting change.

The Science of Influence

Influence is about relationships. It's built on trust, credibility, and respect. Robert Cialdini, in his seminal work Influence: *The Psychology of Persuasion (1984),* identified six principles of influence: reciprocity, commitment, social proof, authority, liking, and scarcity. These principles operate in every context, from business to politics to family life.

For example, the principle of reciprocity, the tendency to return favors, has been shown to increase compliance rates in experiments by as much as 50% (Cialdini, 2001). Social proof, the idea that people follow the actions of others, can drive behaviors ranging from charitable giving to voting.

In the Army, I saw influence at work in the Combined Federal Campaign (CFC). The previous year's campaign had failed, not because of a lack of authority, but because of a lack of buy-in. By building relationships, making the process easier, and showing the importance of the campaign, I was able to inspire even the most skeptical representatives to excel. The result? We not only met our goal, but we exceeded it by nearly six figures.

This story is not unique. Research by Kouzes and Posner (2017) in *The Leadership Challenge* found that leaders who model the way, inspire a shared vision, and enable others to act are far more effective than those who rely on authority alone.

The Limits of Influence

Influence has its limits. It can be undermined by a lack of credibility, trust, or alignment with group values. In the PLDC example, the squad leader who tried to impose changes without regard for the group's established norms lost influence, despite having formal authority. Their power was hollow, and their efforts were resisted.

This dynamic is supported by research on psychological reactance: the tendency for people to resist attempts to control their behavior (Brehm, 1966). When leaders use authority without influence, they often encounter resistance, disengagement, or even sabotage.

Authority: The Formalization of Power

"Authority without wisdom is like a heavy axe without an edge, fitter to bruise than polish." –Anne Bradstreet.

Authority is the formal right to direct, command, or make decisions. It is often tied to position, title, or recognized expertise. In organizations, authority is necessary to maintain order, allocate resources, and ensure accountability.

The Sources of Authority

Max Weber, a foundational sociologist, identified three types of authority (Weber, 1947):

- Traditional Authority: Rooted in customs and long-standing practices.
- Charismatic Authority: Based on personal magnetism and the ability to inspire.
- Legal-Rational Authority: Grounded in formal rules and procedures.

In the Army, authority is clearly defined. Orders, ranks, and roles are set out in regulations. Authority can be delegated, as when a Commander goes on leave and appoints an Acting Commander. However, responsibility cannot be delegated; it remains with the person ultimately accountable.

The Responsibilities of Authority

With authority comes responsibility. Research by Linda Hill (2003) in *Becoming a Manager* found that new managers often struggle with the transition from individual contributor to authority figure. The key challenge is learning to use authority wisely, balancing the need for control with the need to empower others.

Authority can be abused. *The Stanford Prison Experiment (Zimbardo, 1971)* famously demonstrated how quickly people in positions of authority can become abusive when unchecked. This is why checks and balances, transparency, and accountability are essential in any system of authority. Authority, when used well, creates clarity, order, and direction. It enables organizations to function, teams to coordinate, and missions to be accomplished.

The Interplay of Influence and Authority

The most effective leaders combine influence and authority. They use their formal power to set direction and make decisions, but they rely on influence to inspire, persuade, and build commitment.

Research on Leadership Effectiveness

A meta-analysis by Judge et al. (2004) found that transformational leaders, those who inspire and motivate, are more effective than transactional leaders, who rely on authority and rewards.

Transformational leadership is rooted in influence: articulating a vision, modeling desired behaviors, and fostering trust.

In contrast, leaders who rely solely on authority may achieve compliance, but rarely achieve commitment. Gallup's *State of the American Workplace Report (2017)* found that only 33% of employees are engaged at work, with the remainder disengaged or actively disengaged. The primary driver of engagement? Leadership that combines authority with influence.

The Dangers of Power Without Influence

When authority is exercised without influence, it can breed resentment, resistance, and even rebellion. In the PLDC story, the squad leader's authority was undermined by a lack of influence. Research on toxic leadership (Lipman-Blumen, 2005) shows that leaders who rely on coercion, manipulation, or intimidation create environments of fear and disengagement.

Conversely, influence without authority can be equally problematic. The installation commander's spouse wielded significant influence, but without formal authority, their actions could create confusion, resentment, and even undermine the commander's credibility.

The key is balance. The most effective leaders understand when to use authority, when to rely on influence, and how to integrate the two.

Types of Power, Influence, and Authority

To further clarify these concepts, let's look at the different types outlined by organizational psychologists and leadership theorists:

Types of Power (French & Raven, 1959)

- Legitimate Power: Based on position or formal authority.
- Coercive Power: Based on the ability to punish.
- Reward Power: Based on the ability to provide rewards.
- Expert Power: Based on knowledge or expertise.
- Referent Power: Based on personal traits or relationships.
- Informational Power: Based on access to information.

Types of Influence

- Positional Influence: Derived from one's role or title.
- Coercive Influence: Based on threats or punishment.

- Reward Influence: Based on the ability to provide incentives.
- Expert Influence: Based on skills or knowledge.
- Referent Influence: Based on admiration or respect.

Types of Authority (Weber, 1947)

- Traditional Authority: Rooted in customs or longstanding practices.
- Charismatic Authority: Based on personal magnetism.
- Legal-Rational Authority: Based on formal rules and procedures.
- Moral Authority: Based on ethical or moral standing.
- Expert Authority: Based on recognized expertise.

Understanding these distinctions helps clarify why some leaders succeed where others fail, and why some organizations thrive while others falter.

Practical Applications: Building Your Influence and Authority

So, how can you build your influence and authority? Research and experience point to several key strategies:

- **Build Trust and Credibility**

Trust is the foundation of influence. Stephen M.R. Covey, in *The Speed of Trust (2006),* found that high-trust organizations outperform low-trust organizations by nearly 300%. Trust is built through consistency, competence, and integrity.

- **Develop Expertise**

Expert power is one of the most effective forms of influence. A study by the Center for Creative Leadership (2016) found that leaders who are perceived as experts are more likely to be trusted, respected, and followed.

- **Cultivate Relationships**

Influence is relational. Take time to build rapport, listen actively, and understand others' perspectives. Research by Tiziana Casciaro and Miguel Sousa Lobo (*Harvard Business Review, 2005*) found that people are more likely to be influenced by those they like and trust.

- **Use Authority Wisely**

Authority should be exercised with wisdom and humility. Set clear expectations, provide support, and hold people accountable, but avoid micromanagement or coercion.

- **Inspire a Shared Vision**

People are more likely to follow those who articulate a compelling vision and invite others to participate. Kouzes and Posner (2017) found that vision-driven leaders are more effective at motivating and engaging their teams.

Reflection and Self-Assessment

To harness the power of influence and authority, self-awareness is essential. Here are some practical steps you can take:

- **Identify Your Behavioral Style:**
Tools like DISC or the Myers-Briggs Type Indicator (MBTI) can help you understand your strengths and weaknesses. (insert link to purchase)
- **Reflect on Your Use of Power:**
When have you used power effectively? When have you misused it?
- **Assess Your Influence and Authority:**
Where do you have the most influence? Where do you have formal authority? How do these overlap or conflict?
- **Identify Key Influencers in Your Life:**
Who shapes your decisions? Why do you give them that power?
- **Set Goals for Growth:**
Where do you want to increase your influence or authority? What steps can you take to get there?

The Ethical Dimension: Power and Responsibility

"With great power comes great responsibility."

—Voltaire

The ethical use of power is a recurring theme in both philosophy and leadership literature. Research by Hannah, Avolio, and Walumbwa (2011) on moral potency found that leaders who act with moral courage, ownership, and efficacy are more likely to use power for the greater good.

Unchecked power can lead to abuse, corruption, and harm, but power, when guided by strong values and a commitment to service, can transform organizations and societies.

Conclusion: The Call to Lead with Influence and Authority

Influence and authority are the twin engines of power. Used together, they can remove obstacles, create opportunities, and bring people together for a common purpose. Used irresponsibly, they can divide, destroy, and hinder progress.

As you reflect on your journey, consider the following:

- How do you use your influence and authority
- Are you building trust, credibility, and relationships?
- Are you using your authority to empower others or to control them?
- What values guide your use of power?

Leadership is not reserved for those with titles or formal authority. As John Maxwell reminds us, leadership is influence. We all have the power to lead, to shape outcomes, and to make a difference.

My challenge to you is to use the power, influence, and authority entrusted to you to help others, solve problems, and bring more good into the world. Reflect on your strengths and weaknesses, seek feedback, and commit to growing as a leader.

Remember, the true measure of power is not in how much you control, but in how much you empower others.

Call to Action

As you continue your journey, I encourage you to:

- Complete a behavioral assessment (such as

DISC) and reflect on your style's strengths and weaknesses. (www.MyDISCReport.com)

- Identify the areas in your life where your power, influence, and authority are most valuable.
- Consider where you wish you had more power, influence, or authority, and what steps you can take to achieve it.
- Reflect on those who influence you most, and why you grant them that power.
- Commit to using your influence and authority to serve others, solve problems, and make a positive impact.

The world needs leaders who understand the true nature of power, those who blend influence and authority with wisdom, humility, and a commitment to the greater good. Will you answer the call?

CHAPTER 5

LEADERSHIP AT EVERY LEVEL:
YOU DON'T NEED A TITLE TO LEAD

Dr. Katherine Y. Baines Brown

*L*eadership is not about position; it's about posture. It's about how you choose to show up, serve others, and influence outcomes, regardless of where your name falls on your company's organizational chart. Titles can open doors, but character is what keeps them open.

In my experience across public health, academia, nonprofit work, and international leadership, I've learned that the most transformative leaders are not always the ones with the biggest offices. They're the ones who take ownership without being asked, elevate others without being praised, and remain steady without needing the spotlight.

Leadership Redefined

Too often, leadership is defined by rank, title, salary, or tenure, but I've worked with students, interns, medical assistants, medical students, and community workers who led movements without holding a formal title. They lead by influence, by excellence, and by example.

I've also held titles like professor, founder, and director, and I can tell you this: a title will never carry you where your integrity, consistency, and voice are not already going.

Leadership at every level means you understand your presence matters. Whether you're a student leading a group project, an assistant organizing behind the scenes, or a new hire asking good questions in a meeting, you're modeling something, and others are watching.

> **"LEADERSHIP AT EVERY LEVEL MEANS YOU UNDERSTAND YOUR PRESENCE MATTERS."**

So the question becomes: *What are you modeling, and who are you becoming while you model it?*

My Story: Leadership Before the Title "Dr. Katherine"

My leadership began long before the world knew my name. At Chicago Vocational High School, I ranked #2 in the top 10 all-around seniors and was recognized for excellence in academics and the arts. As first chair in the concert band, I proudly performed the piccolo solo in *"The Star-Spangled Banner"* and received the prestigious John Philip Sousa Award. I also won first place in the All -City Solo Competition and was a founding member of the Chicago Teen Ensemble alongside the now-renowned flutist Demarre McGill. Our mutual instructor, Susan Leviton from the Sherwood Conservatory of Music, taught us that discipline and preparation were non-negotiable.

My flute journey began at Samuel Gompers Elementary School under Band Director Mark Jordan. While others had started earlier, I had to dedicate long hours and intense focus to rise to their level, and eventually, surpass it. I juggled responsibilities, rehearsals, leadership, and service from a young age. It was a lot. I was already multitasking before I knew the term; it was simply who I was.

My leadership didn't begin with a title; it began with survival, resilience, and purpose. After graduating from high school at age 17, I became pregnant. At 18, I gave birth to my first child, my son. Many would have counted me out, but I decided that my story wouldn't stop there. I pursued college while raising a child. I earned my bachelor's degree, followed by a master's degree, and eventually completed my doctoral degree by the age of 30.

In my 20s, while raising a growing family, I became a college professor. My title then was not Dr. Brown, it was "Mom," "Ms. Brown," and often simply "the one who shows up." But I led in every space: in the classroom, in faculty meetings, in the community, and at home. I led my children through the values of discipline, service, and belief. I led students by showing them that no matter where you begin, your life can be built with purpose and perseverance.

Before I taught CPR, I knew of CPR from my mother, a nurse. That training sparked a movement. I didn't just learn it, I taught it, lived it, and eventually built a business around it. I went on to found Dr. Katherine and Associates CPR Courses (DK&A), Learn CPR America, LLC, and Dr. KYB Leadership Academy, not because someone permitted me, but because I saw a need.

My leadership extended globally. I've traveled to Trinidad and Tobago, Dubai, Colombia, South Africa, and beyond, training and equipping young people and professionals in leadership, health, and service. Yet, some of my greatest leadership lessons came from within my home: nurturing four children to lead with excellence, empathy, and endurance.

Leadership doesn't require applause. It requires alignment. Before I ever stood on a TEDx stage or received an award, I led by example at home, in classrooms, in churches, and in small moments that mattered.

Upon reflection, I began volunteering and teaching heart health at age 16. I wasn't a doctor of education, a professor, or a keynote speaker, but I knew lives were on the line, and that if I could give people the skills to save a life, I was doing work that mattered. My title was "teenager." My impact was leadership.

> **"LEADERSHIP DOESN'T REQUIRE APPLAUSE. IT REQUIRES ALIGNMENT."**

I didn't wait for permission. I led CPR demonstrations in churches, schools, barber shops, and beauty salons. I founded Learn CPR America before I ever stood behind a podium. My leadership was born from necessity and nurtured through service.

It started when I showed up consistently, mentored others, and served with excellence, even when no one was clapping.

5 Foundations of Leadership at Every Level

1. Initiative Without Instruction

Leadership doesn't wait to be asked. It sees what needs to be done and does it. Some of the strongest leaders I've mentored were the ones who said, "I noticed this could be improved, so I created a draft."

A young student in KYB once noticed our welcome packet needed revision. She took it upon herself to design a clearer, more engaging version. We didn't assign her that task, but she saw a gap and filled it. That was leadership. She later went on to design promotional materials that we still use today.

2. Influence Without Authority

You don't need to sign checks to change culture. Influence is earned through trust, credibility, and how you treat people.

I've seen interns shift team morale just by being consistent and respectful. One intern noticed that staff rarely greeted each other in the morning. She started simply saying "good morning" every day. Within weeks, the tone of the office changed. One small act, repeated with sincerity, shifted the energy of an entire team. That's influence. That's leadership.

3. Integrity Without Oversight

True leaders lead even when no one is watching. They honor their commitments, keep their word, and take responsibility.

A former KYB intern worked remotely for a non-profit partner. She wasn't on campus. No one checked in daily, but she met every deadline, documented every project, and went above and beyond. Her supervisor told me, "She made herself indispensable." That's the kind of integrity that builds trust and future opportunities.

4. Invest in Others Without Agenda

Leadership is service. It's about building others up, not collecting fans.

When I was mentoring a group of college students, one young man began coaching other students on presentation skills. He wasn't asked. He just noticed someone struggling and offered help. Later, when he graduated, three students credited him for their growth. That's leadership that multiplies.

5. Innovation Without Recognition

Real leaders bring solutions, not just problems. They create, they refine, and they help others see what's possible. One KYB student designed a social media plan that increased our engagement by 70%. She didn't ask for credit. She saw a need and solved it. Later, we featured her work at our conference, and she now consults for digital strategy teams. Innovation begins when you stop waiting for credit and start focusing on what could be better.

> "...THE MOST EFFECTIVE LEADERSHIP HAPPENS WHEN YOU LEAD UPWARD."

Leading Upward: Influence Without a Title

Leadership without a title doesn't mean staying silent around those who have one. Some of the most effective leadership happens when you lead upward, influencing those above you with insight, humility, and strategic communication.

To Lead Upward Well:
- Come prepared with facts, not feelings.
- Offer solutions, not just problems.
- Speak with respect, but don't diminish your ideas.

I've had assistants respectfully suggest program changes that dramatically improved our workflow. They didn't need to be in charge; they just needed to be courageous. Remember, you don't need a title to lead upward. You just need clarity, credibility, and care.

Leadership in Digital and Remote Spaces

In today's world, many teams operate virtually. So, how do you lead without a title online?
- Respond promptly and professionally.
- Clarify before assuming.
- Use tone and language that fosters collaboration.
- Offer ideas and support in group chats, emails, and virtual meeting rooms.

I've watched people lead breakout sessions on Zoom simply because they volunteered first. Digital space is a new frontier, and title-free leadership thrives there.

L.E.A.D. Framework: A Model for Everyday Leadership

I use four steps that form the acronym of the L.E.A.D. model in my workshops:

- L – Listen Actively: Great leaders hear what's said, and what's not.
- E – Elevate Others: Celebrate wins, share credit, amplify good work.
- A – Act with Integrity: Keep your word. Own your errors.
- D – Deliver Consistently: Show up on time. Finish what you start.

This model works whether you're leading one person or one hundred. Everyone matters.

Leadership Is a Mirror, Not a Megaphone

One of the challenges of leadership without a title is the temptation to prove yourself, but real leadership isn't loud; it's consistent. It's rooted in reflection, not performance.

I've learned this the hard way. There were times I thought I had to prove my worth to be taken seriously, but what earned me trust wasn't perfection; it was humility. It was owning mistakes, asking questions, and showing up for others. Leadership at every level begins when you stop needing to be seen and start focusing on who you're becoming.

> "LEADERSHIP...BEGINS WHEN YOU STOP NEEDING TO BE SEEN AND START FOCUSING ON WHO YOU ARE BECOMING."

Take a Moment for Reflection + Action.

Use these prompts to apply what you've read:

- List three ways you already lead without a title.
- Identify one area where your consistency can improve.
- Who can you mentor, support, or elevate this month?
- Think of a leader who influenced you without holding a title. What did they do?
- Create your personal "leadership without a title" action plan for the next 30 days.

Consider how you will serve others well, because it's the right thing to do.

Make a Commitment

You don't need a title to:
- Lead a meeting with clarity
- Mentor someone behind you
- Speak up when something isn't right
- Build something that didn't exist before

You just need to choose to lead where you are, with what you have, for the good of those around you. Leadership at every level is not a trend; it's a necessity. Our world needs more people who lead because it's who they are, not because it's what they're called. No title required.

II

Leadership
in
Action

*O*nce the foundation is laid, leadership must be lived. This section moves us from theory to practice, off the page and into real-world situations. Here, we unpack how leadership shows up in decision-making, accountability, coaching, and navigating high-stakes environments.

You'll read about frameworks like MOVE™, discover the power of leading with clarity and empathy, and explore how to foster performance, culture, and trust in a world that is anything but predictable. These chapters offer tools, stories, and insights for the leader who wants to move from good intentions to real impact; every day, for everyone.

Leadership isn't a passive role. It's an active, courageous choice, daily. Let's get into the rhythm of showing up with intention and influence.

CHAPTER 6
COACHING AND MANAGING:
THE COMPLEMENTARY KEYS TO
TEAM SUCCESS

Angela Hooper-Menifield

The Leadership Misstep: When Balance Was Lost

There's been a subtle but significant shift in how we talk about leadership in recent years. Somewhere along the way, "manager" became a dirty word, and "coach" was crowned as the more evolved, enlightened approach. Leadership literature, conferences, and consultants all began championing the message: Don't manage, coach. Don't control, empower. Don't direct, develop.

While I support the intent behind that shift, I've seen firsthand how this binary thinking has created new problems for leaders. In many organizations, leaders, especially new or mid-level ones, were encouraged to coach but never trained to manage well in the first place. Others, trying to keep up with shifting expectations, abandoned the very clarity, structure, and accountability that teams still desperately need.

The result is confused leaders, overwhelmed teams, missed goals, and frustration all around. I've worked with clients, teams, and executives who fell into this trap, not because they were bad leaders, but because they were told that coaching was the gold standard and managing was outdated. In reality, leadership isn't about choosing one over the other. It's about integrating both.

Great leaders don't shy away from managing. They manage well and wisely with structure, direction, and accountability. They coach, intentionally and consistently, to grow people, unlock potential, and build trust. These two skill sets are not at odds. The most effective leaders I've encountered don't see managing and coaching as separate lanes. They see them as complementary tools in their leadership toolkit.

In the chapters of my leadership journey, from managing large federal teams to coaching rising leaders in diverse industries, I've come to this truth: High-performing teams don't need just a manager or a coach. They need a leader who knows when to direct and when to develop. That balance and blend is what this chapter is about.

> "THE MOST EFFECTIVE LEADERS...SEE MANAGING AND COACHING AS...COMPLEMENTARY TOOLS IN THEIR LEADERSHIP TOOLKIT."

Clarifying the Difference, and the Value of Both

One of the biggest barriers to leading effectively is confusion about roles. Too often, leaders are promoted without ever being taught the difference between managing work and developing people. When those distinctions aren't understood, it's easy to default to one and neglect the other. Let's take a moment to define what we mean.

Managing is about providing direction. It ensures that goals are met, resources are aligned, and expectations are clear. It's focused on timelines, outcomes, and accountability. Managing is what keeps the trains running on time.

Coaching, on the other hand, is about developing the person behind the performance. It invites curiosity. It asks questions. It challenges assumptions. Coaching focuses on unlocking potential and empowering people to think, grow, and take ownership.

> **"COACHING IS ABOUT DEVELOPING THE PERSON BEHIND THE PERFORMANCE."**

Here's how I often break it down for the leaders I work with:

Coaching and Managing: A Side-by-Side Breakdown

Managing	Coaching
Directs tasks	Develops people
Focuses on outcomes	Focuses on awareness
Tells and instructs	Asks and listens
Drives performance	Unlocks potential
Immediate execution	Long-term development
Provides direction	Encourages reflection
Solves the problem	Uncovers the root
Delegates tasks	Elevates thinking

Neither is better. Neither is more noble. They simply serve different purposes, and leadership requires both.

Let me be clear: there are moments when a team member needs clear guidance, firm boundaries, and specific instruction. That's not micromanagement. That's management done well. There are also moments when telling isn't what's needed, when the most powerful thing you can do is ask a question, offer a challenge, or create space for reflection. That's where coaching comes in. I often tell the leaders I train: "Management keeps people aligned. Coaching keeps them engaged."

Even more foundational is this: "Direct the task. Develop the person."

When both are in place, people know where they're going and feel empowered in how they get there. That's where trust is built. That's where leadership goes from functional to transformational.

My Turning Point: Adding Coaching to My Toolkit

I've always believed in managing well. Structure, clarity, and accountability have never been optional in my leadership playbook. Those qualities helped me lead large, complex teams during my federal career and continue to anchor the work I do with organizations today.

I think back to when I was leading, directly and indirectly, over 4,000 employees across 14 U.S. locations. There was no room for ambiguity. Managing was essential. Our policies had to be followed. Our expectations had to be clear. Our services had to meet the public standard every single day.

But I'll never forget the moment I realized managing alone wasn't enough. You see, I was working with a highly capable team, yet I could feel that something was off. The metrics looked good on paper, but the engagement was flat. People were meeting expectations, but rarely exceeding them. Ideas were minimal, energy was low, and morale had become... professional, but perfunctory.

One day, during a one-to-one, a high-performing employee I deeply respected said something that stopped me cold. After walking through their quarterly metrics, they paused and said:

"I know I'm doing fine, but I'm not sure I'm growing anymore."

That conversation changed everything. I started small and began intentionally weaving coaching conversations into our structured leadership meetings. I'd ask regional leaders, "What conversations are you having that go beyond deadlines and metrics?" Or, "Who's on your team that might be ready for more, but just hasn't been asked?"

For non-managerial team members, I'd ask, "What's working for you right now, and what's not?" Or, "Where do you feel stretched, and where do you feel stuck?"

I noticed the difference almost immediately. The conversations got richer. My team began showing up with ideas, not just updates. They started asking more of themselves. Perhaps most importantly, they started seeing me not just as the one who set expectations, but as someone invested in their development.

The ultimate, more tangible result was that we started developing bench strength. Leaders who were once only executors became thinkers, innovators, and mentors to others. The blend of clear management and intentional coaching transformed our pipeline.

In my consulting work, I once coached a mid-level manager who was deeply respected but exhausted. She was a checklist champion; her team met deadlines, stayed in compliance, and rarely pushed back. The problem was that they weren't growing, and neither was she.

I worked with her to integrate three simple coaching behaviors into her leadership rhythm:

- Asking more open-ended questions during one-to-ones
- Shifting feedback from correction to reflection
- Making space in meetings for team members to propose, not just report

She didn't stop managing. She still held the line, but within 60 days, engagement on her team improved, collaboration increased, and one employee she thought about letting go became one of her most creative problem-solvers.

The structure stayed. The energy shifted. This manager learned just as I had that this shift didn't water down our leadership; it deepened it. We didn't stop managing. We expanded our approach, and that expansion changed everything.

Knowing When to Coach and When to Manage

One of the most important leadership skills isn't just knowing how to coach or manage, it's knowing when to do each. Too many leaders default to one style, regardless of the situation. They either manage everything, micromanaging progress and stifling initiative, or coach everything, asking endless questions when what's needed is a firm decision and direction.

Effective leadership is about reading the moment, the mission, and the maturity of the person in front of you. Here's how I help leaders find that balance. When faced with a challenge or decision, ask yourself:

3 Coaching vs. Managing Questions:
1. **Does this moment require clarity or curiosity?** If the person is unsure about expectations, deliverables, or boundaries, manage. If they know what's required but need to build capacity or confidence, you should coach.
2. **Is the priority performance or potential?** Managing ensures the current objective is achieved. Coaching focuses on future growth and skill-building. Sometimes both are needed, just not in the same moment.
3. **Do they need direction or discovery?** A new employee may need firm guidance. A seasoned team member might benefit more from reflective space.

Practical Examples from the Field

Managing Moment:

A team is struggling to meet a time-sensitive deliverable. The client's deadline is non-negotiable. In this case, you don't pause for a coaching session. You manage the moment, assign roles, set check-in times, clarify non-negotiables, and push for execution.

Coaching Moment:

You notice one team member consistently hesitating during meetings. Their performance is fine, but they seem disengaged or unsure. This is the moment to ask:

- "I've noticed you're a bit quieter lately. What's going on beneath the surface?"
- "What would make you feel more confident in this space?"

There's no one-size-fits-all answer. Discernment is the leadership superpower. When leaders learn to toggle between coaching and managing based on the needs of the situation and the people involved, they create teams that are not only effective but also empowered. Coaching grows capacity. Managing protects clarity. Leadership requires both.

Adding Coaching to Everyday Leadership

One of the most common myths I hear is, "I don't have time to coach. I barely have time to manage."

But the truth is, coaching isn't something you schedule once a quarter. It's something you integrate into how you lead every day. You don't have to host a 90-minute development session to be a coach. You simply have to shift the way you show up in conversations, meetings, and even quick hallway check-ins. Small changes in your questions, your listening, and your presence can spark big growth over time.

I learned this firsthand in my federal leadership role. When you're leading thousands of employees across multiple states, time is a luxury. However, I knew that if I wanted to build a team of independent thinkers and not just task completers, I had to be intentional about how I communicated. So, I started using coaching practices in the middle of the work, not in place of it. It changed everything.

Here are three ways I help leaders bring coaching into their everyday leadership, just like I did for myself then and how I do now with many of my clients.

1. Ask Before You Answer.
Instead of jumping in with solutions, pause and ask:
- *"What have you already tried?"*
- *"What do you think would work best here?"*

I used this often during my team's planning meetings. People would come to me expecting decisions, but I'd flip it. I'd ask them what they would do if they were sitting in my seat. Nine times out of ten, they had the right idea, they just needed the confidence to voice it.

This simple shift not only empowered them, but it also freed me from being the bottleneck in every decision.

2. Turn Feedback into Reflection.
Don't just correct behavior, invite awareness. Instead of, "Next time, copy me on the report."
Try:
"Let's walk through that moment. What do you think worked well, and what might you do differently next time?"

I once had a direct report who struggled with presenting updates confidently. Rather than critique his delivery, I asked: "How did that feel to you?"

That opened the door to a bigger conversation about

confidence, preparation, and even imposter syndrome. That moment wouldn't have happened if I had defaulted to fixing instead of coaching.

3. Use One-to-ones For Growth, Not Just Updates.

Too many leaders spend check-ins reviewing what's already happened. Coaching-minded leaders ask:

- "Where do you feel most energized, and where are you stuck?"
- "What's a skill or area you'd like to strengthen this quarter?"

During my consulting with organizations today, I help leaders redesign their one-to-ones around these kinds of questions. One client told me it completely transformed how his team showed up. What used to be a 20-minute status report became a meaningful, strategic conversation that reconnected people to their purpose, not just their tasks.

> "COACHING DOESN'T REPLACE PERFORMANCE; IT ENHANCES IT."

These micro-moments don't take more time. They take more intention. The return on that intention? Loyalty, creativity, and leadership maturity across your team.

Coaching doesn't replace performance; it enhances it. It keeps your team learning, engaged, and evolving, even as you continue to manage outcomes with clarity.

If I've learned anything over the years, it's this: when you care enough to develop someone, they care more about delivering results. That's the kind of culture coaching creates, one conversation at a time.

A Story of Dual Impact

Early in my career, I had a team member who was extremely competent. She was one of those people who you just knew would get the job done. She hit her deadlines, kept her reports accurate, and never needed to be reminded of what was expected. From a management perspective, she was a dream.

But something didn't sit right with me. Despite her performance, she rarely spoke up in meetings. She deferred to others even when she had better insights. And while she never said it out loud, I could see it: she was playing small.

I could have kept managing her the way I always had: acknowledging her output, thanking her for her consistency, and leaving it at that, but I knew there was more in her. I knew that if I didn't coach it out, it might never surface.

So I changed my approach. In our next one-to-one, I asked her a different kind of question:

"What would stepping into the next level of leadership look like for you?"

She looked at me, surprised. No one had ever asked her that. That conversation opened the door. I found out she had ideas to streamline a process we were spending hours on every week. She had been sitting on it, unsure if she had the "authority" to share. I gave her the space to present it at our next leadership meeting, and it worked. We saved time, money, and her confidence skyrocketed.

But here's the thing: I still managed her. I still held her accountable for her performance. I didn't replace management with coaching; I layered coaching on top of it. Because of that, I didn't just get a dependable employee, I got a growing leader.

Fast forward to my consulting practice years later, and the same principle continues to hold. I worked with a client who led a large operations team. He was highly respected, efficient, and known for "getting things done." But his team operated like task rabbits, minimal engagement, minimal input. People did their jobs, but they didn't own them. When I introduced him to the coaching model, he was skeptical. "I don't have time for therapy sessions," he joked.

I encouraged him to start small. In his next one-to-ones, I asked him to close the laptop and ask his team members, "What's something you're proud of this week that I might not know about?"

Within three weeks, everything shifted. His team started speaking up in meetings. One person was asked to lead a project. Another offered feedback that improved a workflow. He realized he wasn't just managing, he was creating engagement through development.

That's what I mean by dual impact. When we coach and manage together, we don't just move work forward, we move people forward. That is what high-performing, high-trust teams are built on.

Leading with Both: Final Reflection

At this stage in my career, I've seen leadership evolve. I've also seen where it's gotten off track. Somewhere along the line, we were taught to choose management or coaching, to be the rule-setter or the motivator, the driver or the developer. Real leadership has never been about choosing one over the other. It's about knowing when to lead with direction and when to lean in with development. It's about using discernment, emotional intelligence, and situational awareness to bring out the best in others and yourself.

If all you ever do is manage, your team may comply, but they won't grow. If all you ever do is coach, your team may feel supported, but they won't be aligned. The magic happens when you do both.

> **"IF ALL YOU EVER DO IS MANAGE, YOUR TEAM MAY COMPLY, BUT THEY WON'T GROW."**

What the Research Shows

This dual-path approach isn't just my experience; it's backed by data from some of the world's most respected leadership studies:

- Gallup found that managers who coach their teams (vs. only manage) see a 21% boost in productivity, and employees who receive weekly coaching feedback are 3x more engaged (Gallup, 2015).
- Google's Project Oxygen ranked "Is a good coach" as the #1 trait of high-performing managers, above technical skills or subject matter expertise (Google, re: Work).
- McKinsey & Company found that leaders who combine directive management and supportive coaching boost employee satisfaction by 40% and team performance by 25% (McKinsey, 2022).
- Deloitte's 2023 Human Capital Trends report revealed that high-performing organizations are 2x

more likely to train managers in both coaching and performance management strategies (Deloitte, 2023).

The leaders who get this right don't just lead high-performing teams; they build cultures where people think, stretch, and thrive.

So let me ask you:

- Where in your leadership are you over-indexing on one style and underusing the other?
- Who on your team needs clearer expectations from you right now?
- Who might flourish if you simply asked a better question instead of answering?

You don't need to overhaul your leadership style. You just need to bring awareness and intentionality to how you show up.

- Start small.
- Ask one reflective question in your next meeting.
- Shift one piece of feedback from correction to curiosity.
- Revisit a process not just for what's working, but for who's growing.

When you direct the task and develop the person, you're not just doing leadership right, you're doing leadership that lasts.

CHAPTER 7

THE MOVE™ FRAMEWORK FOR LEADERSHIP SUCCESS

Angela Hooper-Menifield

*T*he ability to grow as a leader isn't just about what you do, it's about how you move through change, challenge, and opportunity.

Why Leaders Need a Framework to Move Forward

Leadership is often romanticized as vision casting, decision-making, or standing at the front of the room with all the answers. In reality, leadership is movement. It's about knowing how to navigate uncertainty, guide others through complexity, and keep going when the way forward isn't clear.

Over the years, I've worked with leaders across industries, ages, and titles, from those managing their first teams to those running entire agencies or companies. The same truth shows up again and again: leadership stalls when movement stops.

Sometimes the obstacle is fear. Sometimes it's indecision. Sometimes it's just the pace of change, but no matter the reason, the result is the same: good people with great potential get stuck.

I created the MOVE™ Framework to help leaders break through that stuckness, not just to act, but to act with alignment. Whether you're navigating a career pivot, guiding a team through transition, or simply trying to grow into the next version of yourself, MOVE™ gives you a map.

MOVE™ stands for:
- M – Mindset
- O – Options
- V – Vision
- E – Execution

Each element is a leadership muscle, and when developed together, they create the kind of leader who doesn't just survive change but leads others confidently through it.

This chapter isn't about theory. It's about practice. It starts with the foundation of it all: your mindset.

M is for Mindset: Leading from the Inside Out

Leadership doesn't start with strategy. It starts with belief: what you believe about yourself, your people, and what's possible.

That's why the first phase of the *MOVE*™ Framework is Mindset. Before you take action, cast vision, or explore your options, you have to check the internal engine that's driving your decisions.

> **"LEADERSHIP DOESN'T START WITH STRATEGY. IT STARTS WITH BELIEF."**

You will never lead further than your mindset allows you to go.

This isn't just about confidence or positivity; it's about awareness. Leaders must become fluent in recognizing the narratives they carry. Are you operating from a place of fear or faith, scarcity or possibility? Do you believe your voice matters? Do you believe people can change? Do you believe you can?

I've worked with high-level professionals whose credentials were impeccable, but they still led from a place of fear. They avoided difficult conversations, micromanaged their teams, or stayed stuck in roles they'd outgrown because their internal mindset said: Play it safe. Don't risk it. This is enough.

Mindset shows up in how we respond to feedback. Whether we seek collaboration or control. Whether we see problems or possibilities.

Case in Point: Howard Schultz – Reimagining Leadership Through Belief

Howard Schultz wasn't born into wealth. Raised in public housing in Brooklyn, his leadership journey was shaped not by entitlement but by vision. When he first joined Starbucks in the 1980s, it was a small Seattle coffee chain. Schultz saw something others didn't: a belief that coffee could become an experience, not just a transaction.

That belief led him to buy the company and transform it. What's often overlooked is what happened years later, when Starbucks faced declining performance and cultural erosion.

In 2008, Schultz made a bold decision: he returned as CEO, not just to manage operations, but to reset the mindset of the company.

- He closed 7,100 stores for a day to retrain baristas on espresso fundamentals, signaling that excellence and connection mattered more than profit margins.

- He invested in employee benefits during a financial crisis.
- He doubled down on values, not shortcuts.

That wasn't just strategy, it was leadership rooted in mindset:

- People over profit.
- Long-term trust over short-term gain.
- Courage to course-correct instead of coasting.

His leadership became a case study in how belief drives business reinvention. Starbucks didn't just bounce back; it became stronger, more intentional, and more human.

Leadership Reflection:

Before moving into options, ask yourself:

- What belief is currently driving my leadership?
- Where am I leading from fear instead of vision?
- What would shift if I led from a mindset of growth, courage, and trust?

Mindset isn't a box to check. It's a pattern you shape and a foundation you strengthen daily. The leader you are internally will always shape the results you create externally.

O is for Options: Leadership Is a Choice, Not a Script

Once you've shifted your mindset, the next move is unlocking your options. As leaders, we often say we want innovation, flexibility, and progress, but when it's time to choose a path forward, we get stuck in binary thinking. We frame everything as either/or:

- Either I delegate, or I do it myself.
- Either we stay the course, or we blow it all up.
- Either I lead with heart, or I lead with results.

Real leadership isn't about clinging to black-and-white answers. It's about learning to operate in the gray, where creativity, resourcefulness, and growth live. The second phase of the MOVE™ Framework, Options, is where the leader starts leading.

Options Are About Expanding Possibility

In coaching, I see this all the time: brilliant leaders show up with tunnel vision, convinced there's only one viable solution. The moment I slow the conversation and ask, "What else could be true?" or "If you weren't worried about failing, what would you do?", something powerful happens.

They start seeing possibilities instead of problems.

They stop reacting and start reframing.

They stop managing fear and start managing choice.

When you permit yourself to explore options:

- You interrupt limiting beliefs.
- You take ownership of your role in shaping the future.
- You lead with curiosity instead of control.

This phase isn't about having the perfect plan. It's about being willing to step out of autopilot long enough to ask, "What else could I do that aligns with my values, my goals, and my long-term vision?"

When Leaders Avoid Options...

Here's what I've seen in organizations, and maybe you've seen it too:

- A high-potential team member is underperforming, but no one wants to address it, so the entire team suffers.
- A department is misaligned, but the leader keeps trying to fix it with more meetings, instead of reimagining how the work gets done.
- A new idea is brought to the table, but it gets shut down because "that's not how we've done things before."

In each case, the issue isn't a lack of intelligence; it's a lack of optional thinking. Leaders feel boxed in, afraid to challenge the status quo, or too overwhelmed to pause and reflect. When you do pause, take a breath, and explore options, you expand the map.

Leading with Options Looks Like:

- Brainstorming before deciding: "What are 3 paths we haven't explored yet?"
- Using questions to drive clarity: "What would success look like if we approached this differently?"
- Involving multiple perspectives: "Who sees

something I don't see here?"

- Weighing choices beyond ease or speed: "Which option aligns most with our values, even if it's harder?"

Leadership Reflection:
- Where in your leadership have you narrowed your thinking too quickly?
- Are you solving the right problem, or just the most obvious one?
- Have you created a team culture where new ideas are welcomed or quietly avoided?

Leadership is not about having all the answers; it's about being bold enough to explore them.

V is for Vision: Defining the Destination Before You Lead

Once your mindset is aligned and you've explored your options, the next leadership move is to choose a direction with intention.

That's what Vision is all about, the "V" in the MOVE™ Framework.

Vision is not about having all the answers. It's about naming a compelling 'why' that moves you, and moves others.

As a leader, your vision must be more than a quarterly goal or a project deadline. It's the larger destination you're moving toward. It gives your decisions meaning, rallies your team around a purpose, and serves as a compass when things get foggy or frustrating.

Without vision, people don't just wander; they disengage.

Vision Brings Alignment and Energy

I've seen organizations with brilliant people, generous budgets, and strong brand reputations stall out, not because of incompetence, but because the leader never made the vision clear.

> **"WITHOUT VISION, PEOPLE DON'T JUST WANDER; THEY DISENGAGE."**

- Sometimes that's because they assumed everyone already knew it.
- Sometimes it's because the leader hadn't clarified it for themselves.
- Sometimes, let's be honest, it's because the leader was reacting to tasks instead of rising to purpose.

But when leaders pause to define vision:
- Decision-making becomes faster and more focused.
- Morale improves because people know where they're headed.
- Strategy becomes clearer because the outcomes are connected to something bigger.

A vision doesn't have to be grandiose. It just has to be true, to you, your mission, and the people you serve.

Defining Your Leadership Vision

This phase of the MOVE™ Framework invites leaders to move beyond reactive execution and into intentional leadership design. It's where you ask yourself questions like:

- What do I want to be known for?
- What impact do I want my team or organization to make?
- What does success look like beyond the metrics?

In coaching, I often say: "If you can't name the destination, how can you evaluate whether you're making progress?"

Vision vs. Goals: Know the Difference

Goals	Vision
Specific, measurable outcomes	Broad, purpose-driven destination
Often short to medium term	Long-term, enduring focus
Drive tactical decisions	Shape strategic direction
Can change with conditions	Anchors your leadership in meaning

Many leaders confuse goals with vision. They're related, but not the same.
Example:

- A goal might be to increase customer retention by 15%.
- A vision could be to create the most trusted client experience in your industry.

The goal supports the vision, but the vision fuels everything else.

Leadership Reflection:
- Can I clearly articulate my leadership vision in one sentence?
- Does my team know it, and see how their work connects to it?
- Do my daily decisions align with the vision I say matters most?

Coaching Insight:
When you feel distracted or off-track as a leader, don't start with your to-do list. Start with your why. Reconnect to your vision and let it filter your focus. When vision is clear, alignment follows, and execution becomes meaningful, not just mandatory.

"People don't buy what you do, they buy why you do it." – Simon Sinek.

That's true in business, and it's true in leadership.

E is for Execution: Turning Clarity into Consistent Action

You've done the inner work on mindset. You've explored the possible pathways. You've anchored your leadership in a compelling vision. Now comes the part that separates intention from impact: Execution.

Execution is where your leadership shows up, not just in what you say, but in what you do, consistently and with integrity.

In my experience coaching leaders and building organizations, I've seen many people talk like leaders and even think like leaders, but still fall short when it comes to follow-through. Not because they didn't care and not because they weren't capable, but because they lacked the systems, structure, and discipline that execution demands.

Execution Requires Alignment, Not Just Hustle

Too often, we confuse being busy with being productive, but leadership execution isn't about doing more; it's about doing what matters most, consistently.

Execution is about:
- Translating vision into strategy.
- Building habits that support long-term growth.
- Prioritizing without burning out.
- Following through when motivation fades.

This is where the MOVE™ Framework becomes more than insight, and it becomes muscle memory. Execution isn't just a phase. It's a practice.

3 Things Leaders Must Master to Execute Effectively:

1. Clear Prioritization

If everything is urgent, nothing is. You must decide what deserves your best energy, and say no to what doesn't serve the vision.

2. Consistent Follow-Through

Execution is built on trust. People will follow a leader who keeps their word. Don't overpromise. Deliver consistently.

3. Feedback Loops

Execution isn't one-and-done. Smart leaders track what's working, adjust what's not, and invite feedback along the way.

Execution Tools I Recommend to Clients
- Weekly CEO Time: Block 60–90 minutes per week to step out of the weeds and work *on the business, not in it.*
- Priority 3 Framework: Start each day by naming your top 3 outcomes, not tasks, that move the needle.
- Accountability Check-ins: Use coaching-style questions with your team to keep goals visible and shared:
  o "What's your focus this week?"
  o "What's blocking progress?"
  o "What will success look like by Friday?"

Leadership Reflection:
- Am I executing in alignment with my vision or just reacting to whatever shows up?
- What habits or distractions are sabotaging my follow-through?
- Do I have systems that support sustainable progress?

"Vision without execution is just hallucination."

– Thomas Edison

Leadership execution is not about perfection. It's about showing up consistently, with clarity, courage, and commitment.

When you execute well, you build momentum. When you build momentum, you build confidence. Confident leaders move others because they model what it looks like to move forward on purpose.

Integration: How It All Connects

The true power of the MOVE™ Framework doesn't lie in treating each pillar as a separate concept. It comes alive when you see how these elements interact, support one another, and build momentum together.

Mindset without execution is inspiration with no traction. Vision without options becomes rigid and unrealistic. Options without mindset can lead to scattered, unfocused effort. It's not about mastering one piece; it's about creating alignment across all four.

Let's revisit the sequence:

1. Mindset grounds your leadership. It asks: What beliefs are driving me?
2. Options expand your possibilities. It asks: What else is possible?
3. Vision gives you direction. It asks: Where am I going, and why?
4. Execution delivers results. It asks: How will I make it real or tangible?

When these work in harmony, something shifts. Leadership becomes less reactive and more responsive. Less driven by pressure and more driven by purpose.

MOVE™ Is a Cycle, Not a One-Time Event

One of the most important insights I share with clients is that MOVE™ is iterative. You don't go through the four steps once and call it done. Every time a new challenge arises, a new opportunity emerges, or a new season begins, you move through the cycle again.

Some of the best leaders I know revisit this framework monthly, quarterly, or even weekly, asking:

- What needs to shift in my mindset?
- Are there new options I haven't explored?
- Is my vision still relevant and clear?
- What's my plan for execution this week?

That's the beauty of a framework: it keeps you anchored when the world keeps changing.

Real Leadership Application

Here's how a leader might apply MOVE™ in a real-world situation:

Let's say you're navigating a team restructuring:

- Mindset: Acknowledge the fear and uncertainty, then lead with belief in your people and values.
- Options: Consider different structures, timelines, or ways to communicate, not just the default approach.
- Vision: Clearly define what success looks like on the other side of change.
- Execution: Create a transparent plan, set milestones, assign roles, and keep communication flowing.

This model gives you structure without rigidity, clarity without control.

Leadership Reflection:
- Which phase of MOVE™ do I naturally lean into, and which one do I avoid?
- How often do I revisit all four phases in my leadership rhythm?
- How can I use this framework with my team, not just for myself?

When you MOVE™ as a leader, with Mindset, Options, Vision, and Execution in sync, you don't just get results, you create transformation.

You lead with intention.

You grow with integrity.

You build trust, resilience, and momentum, not just for yourself, but for everyone you serve.

The Leader's Call to MOVE™

Leadership isn't static. It's not a title you receive or a box you check. Leadership is a dynamic journey that demands clarity, courage, and consistent movement.

That's why I created the MOVE™ Framework, not as a trendy acronym or another tool to collect dust, but as a practical, repeatable guide for navigating real-world leadership. No matter your industry, your title, or your

> "LEADERSHIP IS A DYNAMIC JOURNEY THAT DEMANDS CLARITY, COURAGE, AND CONSISTENT MOVEMENT."

level of experience, the truth is this: You are always one MOVE™ away from unlocking your next level of leadership.

Why MOVE™ Matters Now

We're living and leading in a time of accelerated change, where certainty is rare, complexity is constant, and leadership fatigue is real. Many leaders feel pulled in a hundred directions, managing expectations, performance, and people, all while trying to stay inspired themselves. In that environment, it's easy to drift, operate on autopilot, and rely on outdated strategies that no longer serve you. That's where the MOVE™ Framework comes in. It's not here to replace your experience; it's here to elevate it, offer structure without rigidity, and to give you a place to pause, reflect, and lead on purpose.

> **"MINDSET WITHOUT EXECUTION IS INSPIRATION WITH NO TRACTION."**

A Leadership Practice, Not a Leadership Theory

Here's how I encourage you to integrate MOVE™ into your rhythm:

- Mindset Check: Start each month with a journal prompt: What belief is driving my leadership right now?
- Options Session: In team meetings, ask: What new possibilities haven't we explored yet?
- Vision Reset: Quarterly, revisit your personal or team vision. Ask: Does this still reflect where we're going?
- Execution Pulse: Weekly, name 1–3 aligned actions that move the vision forward, and follow through.

MOVE™ is not just a framework; it's a leadership habit, one that builds trust, resilience, and intentional growth.

Your MOVE, Your Power

The best leaders I know don't just manage outcomes, they design impact. They don't wait for the perfect moment; they move with clarity, courage, and conviction. Whether you're at the

> **"THE BEST LEADERS... DON'T JUST MANAGE OUTCOMES, THEY DESIGN IMPACT."**

beginning of a new chapter or standing at a professional crossroads, the question is the same:

What's your next MOVE™?

- Will you shift your mindset?
- Explore a new set of options?
- Clarify your vision?
- Finally, take that bold step toward execution?

Whatever it is, don't wait. Your MOVE is your power.

Final Reflection Questions:

- What part of the MOVE™ Framework do I need to lean into right now?
- What would change if I applied it not just at work, but in life?
- What's the one action I'll take this week to MOVE™ forward with intention?

Lead well. Move forward. Real leadership doesn't just react, it responds. It reframes. It moves.

CHAPTER 8

DECISION MAKING UNDER PRESSURE:
LEADING IN UNCERTAINTY

Dr. Tsitsi Hungwe

I've come to believe that the greatest pressure in leadership isn't external, it's internal. It's the pressure of not knowing what's next, yet still feeling like a decision has to be made. The sense that standing still isn't an option, even when the next step isn't fully clear. It's the pressure to decide without a full blueprint, to choose between comfort and calling, stability and possibility.

I witnessed this as a child in the early 2000s, watching my father make the bold decision to resign from the university where he was teaching in Zimbabwe, a move some questioned. A friend mentioned an open position at a university in Michigan. Initially, my father had different plans for his future, but he applied anyway. He trusted what he couldn't yet see and stepped out in faith. He got the job, and that decision changed the trajectory of our family. His choice taught me early on that leadership doesn't require certainty, just the willingness to act.

Nearly two decades later, in 2021, living in Minnesota as a full-time practicing dentist, I found myself in the middle of what I now recognize as an identity crisis. I felt unsure, lost, and quietly questioning my path. I didn't have a plan. I felt stuck, bound by my own limiting beliefs, and searching for a new direction. I didn't know what the next step was, but I knew something had to change. I needed to understand why I was here and what I was meant to do. What I did have was the willingness to take the next step, even without clarity. That posture became the foundation for how I now lead and live.

Sometimes, the answers to our prayers come in a moment and through the people with whom we cross paths. On Juneteenth 2021, I attended *Connect & Collab*, an event hosted by the Black Entrepreneurs Institute. I had been invited by one of the former co-founders. I didn't know anyone else attending, but I was drawn to the energy and authenticity of the space.

During a breakout session, I met Cedrick LaFleur and later added him on Facebook. That simple connection planted a seed. Through Cedrick, I was introduced to Dr. Nicole (Dr. Nic) Rankine, whose guidance would become instrumental in my journey. In the months ahead, I would meet Angela Hooper-Menifield, completing the trio of mentors who would help shape my path.

A few months after *Connect & Collab*, I came across the Business Bootcamp website launched by Cedrick, Dr. Nic, and Angela. They were gearing up for a new cohort that fall. As I read through the site, most of the business terminology went over my head. I felt myself spiraling into analysis paralysis.

"This isn't what a dentist does. Should I even be considering this? Do you have time for this?"

It felt off-script, but deep down, I knew I needed something different. Something kept me gazing at that website. I paused and said to myself,

"What do you have to lose, Tsitsi? Maybe just take it as a class... or a hobby... and learn something new."

So, I signed up one evening. A few days before the first session, I reached out to Angela on Facebook Messenger to introduce myself and let her know I wouldn't be able to attend all of Tuesday's session due to work, but would catch the recordings. She replied warmly and said she was looking forward to getting to know me.

I kept my camera on during the Bootcamp, even though I was camera-shy. Each week, I chose to trust the process, and in doing so, I began to feel my confidence grow. In many ways, the Bootcamp elevated not just my confidence but also my awareness of my boundless potential. I remember thinking, "These people seem helpful and kind. They genuinely want to help me."

I couldn't fully explain why I had joined at the time; it felt like an out-of-body experience, the kind you only understand in hindsight, but something kept nudging me to keep showing up every week.

Week by week, I went from having no background knowledge to slowly gaining clarity and confidence about starting a business. A few weeks in, I had my first one-to-one coaching call with Angela. It was our first conversation outside the larger group, and she helped me think through things I hadn't even found the language for yet.

I would email the co-founders my questions, and Angela would often respond with thoughtful feedback to help me complete my homework. Eventually, I found myself sending her updates through Facebook Messenger, too.

Somewhere along the way, I discovered she was also

an introvert. She shared that openly, and it made me feel more comfortable, seen, and like I could bring my full self into this new space. That sense of belonging and support deepened my engagement.

Over the 60 days in the Bootcamp, I created my business from scratch. I did the work, trusting the process. My business logo was finalized with feedback from my peers and mentors in that very program.

I planned to finish the Bootcamp and move on, to check the box and move forward, but something unexpected happened. The sixty-day experience pulled me in, challenged me, and opened my eyes to possibilities I hadn't considered. I'm grateful to the co-founders for creating a space where I could not only learn business principles but also begin to imagine a new version of myself.

What started as "just something to do" ended up giving me so much more: clarity, deep connection, mentorship, and the courage to launch Higher Mountaintops, LLC, in 2021. Today, I serve as its Chief Executive Officer, helping early professional women find the clarity and confidence to take the next step in their careers.

By 2022, I saw the results of that decision begin to unfold. I spoke on multiple platforms and began growing my business. I called it my "Year of Yes": yes to growth, yes to purpose, yes to becoming. Each "yes" was a decision that helped me thrive, even in the uncertainty of what was next.

What few people know is what happened after that year. In early 2023, I returned from two weeks visiting family in Zimbabwe. At first, I assumed the uneasiness I felt was jet lag or homesickness, but I soon realized the pause had created space to reflect.

Is this still what I want to do?

I felt the full weight of the momentum I had built. I was working part-time as a dentist and running a growing business. I began to question whether I had stepped too far, too soon, too far outside the mold of who I thought I was supposed to be.

Could I keep up the pace? Was I still in alignment? I felt stuck, not from a lack of progress, but because I didn't know how to carry the success. That moment helped me name what I was carrying: pressure. I carried that pressure, even as I accomplished more. Pressure doesn't always come from struggle; sometimes it comes from success.

> "EVEN WHEN YOU'RE PHYSICALLY MOVING FORWARD, IT CAN TAKE MUCH LONGER FOR YOUR MIND AND EMOTIONS TO CATCH UP."

I remember spinning in circles with my coach, Dr. Nicole Rankine, during numerous coaching sessions. I didn't want to quit, but I didn't know if I wanted to keep pushing either. It was like I had hit a wall when I thought I'd have it all figured out.

As high achievers, we're often trained to avoid mistakes. We freeze. We overthink. We default to safe but unfulfilling choices. We wait for the perfect moment instead of choosing what's faithful and right for now.

What I've learned is that even when you're physically moving forward, it can take much longer for your mind and emotions to catch up. I was questioning myself: Was this really what I was supposed to be doing?

When I shared with Angela how I was feeling, she responded with grace and understanding:

"Thank you for your transparency," she said. "For me, it's not uncommon to have moments where, even while excited, I feel like I don't want to do something. It's not necessarily bad."

In another conversation, she added, "Fear isn't an indicator of your inability to do something; it often just means you haven't done it yet. You've got this."

Around that time, she hosted a six-figure mentorship call that I watched on replay. She vulnerably shared how she would download her coach's teachings and listen to them while flying. During tough moments, simply hearing his voice, even through a recording, had helped her stay grounded. I remember thinking, Wow! Wouldn't it be something if I could hear something that resonated with me like that someday?

Not long after, in a quiet moment of reflection, I stumbled upon Angela's TEDx talk, *"Time to Move On"* on YouTube. It spoke directly to what I was feeling, helping me realize that what I was going through wasn't failure, it was transition.

That moment was pivotal. Later, after several clarity coaching sessions with Dr. Nicole, I made a decision: I would step into a new chapter of my life. I would become a career transition coach for early professional women, those starting, advancing, or pivoting in their careers.

Decision Making Under Pressure Is Part of Every Leadership Journey

Learning to thrive in uncertainty isn't about having it

all figured out. It's about having the courage to keep going anyway.

The C.A.L.M.™ Model

To support early professional women navigating transitions, I created the C.A.L.M.™ Model:

- Clarity – Get clear on what you want, not what others expect.
- Assess Options – Identify your choices, uncover what's holding you back, and get the guidance you need to move forward.
- Lean Into Fear – Unpack the fears and limiting beliefs that have kept you stuck in indecision.
- Move with Intention – Take action and create a career success plan.

I lived this model before I had words for it. I found clarity. I sought help. I leaned into fear. I chose to move, even when I didn't feel ready. Here's what I know now: the most defining decisions often happen in moments that don't feel glamorous or decisive at all. They happen in the quiet, in the questioning, and in the "yes" whispered through uncertainty. I spent a long time searching for a blueprint, until I realized: I was the blueprint.

I've learned that the most defining decisions often happen when you least feel ready. The heart of decision-making under pressure is the willingness to act without all the answers, and the strength to trust your inner voice. I wasn't off track. I was right where I was supposed to be: learning to lead through pressure and thrive in uncertainty.

Here's what I know now: had I quit, many people whose lives I've touched since starting Higher Mountaintops, LLC would have missed out—people who were waiting on the other side of my "yes," people who needed what I carry. Leadership means making decisions not just for ourselves, but for the people connected to our choices, those whose growth, breakthroughs, or clarity are waiting on the other side of our obedience. Thriving in uncertainty means showing up, even when you can't see the full impact you're about to make.

> **"THRIVING IN UNCERTAINTY MEANS SHOWING UP, EVEN WHEN YOU CAN'T SEE THE FULL IMPACT YOU'RE ABOUT TO MAKE."**

As I reflect on my journey, I now see how each decision, often made under pressure and uncertainty, played a powerful role in helping me grow, evolve, and ultimately thrive on the other side of every courageous yes. At the time, the steps didn't always make sense, but looking back, the big picture is clear. I was meant to attend *Connect & Collab*. I was meant to join the Bootcamp. I was meant to meet the three mentors who would shape the next chapter of my life far beyond the 60 days we spent together.

Cedrick LaFleur became a trusted mentor I could lean on, sharing invaluable business insights and helping me reconnect with joy through his humor, energy, and deep belief in what's possible. He showed me that leadership can be both purposeful and lighthearted.

Dr. Nicole Rankine became my coach, walking with me through seasons of personal growth while helping me sharpen my vision and expand my business.

Angela Hooper-Menifield became not only a mentor but family. By 2022, I was visiting her and being welcomed into her home and heart as one of her own.

Their care, encouragement, and belief in me have meant more than they may ever realize. Had I not said yes to myself and invested in that Bootcamp, even without knowing all the details, I wouldn't have built this business, met these mentors, or received the unexpected and enduring gift of the Menifield family's love and connection.

That one decision led to more than just professional clarity. It became a personal turning point, a season of doing the self-work, of finding belonging, and of growing into someone equipped to help others through their chapters of uncertainty. Saying yes to something unfamiliar, imperfect, and unclear created the conditions for transformation. Otherwise, I might have remained stuck at a crossroads, circling in doubt.

> **"SAYING YES TO SOMETHING UNFAMILIAR, IMPERFECT, AND UNCLEAR CREATED THE CONDITIONS FOR TRANSFORMATION."**

I chose to move, and that has made all the difference.

The Coaching Edge: How I Help Others Decide

You can't lead people where you haven't gone. My choice to become a coach is grounded in lived experience, self-work, and professional growth, and it's my way of giving back. My journey through uncertainty, pressure, and reinvention led me to this work. I know what it's like to sit in the fog, to feel the pressure of getting it right, of holding it all together, and of wondering whether the path you're walking is still the right one.

This is why I support early professional women through the very steps I once had to take myself:

- Breaking free from analysis paralysis: I've been there, trapped in the swirl of "what-ifs," overthinking every move. I help women move past the many voices, including fear, and take a clear next step.
- Making bold, aligned moves: I know what it's like to do something that doesn't fit the mold. I help early professional women make value-based decisions that reflect not just where they've been, but who they want to become.
- Building self-trust in the unknown: Together, we untangle the limiting beliefs that hold them back and strengthen their ability to lead themselves first.
- Redefining success: Sometimes we chase a version of success that no longer fits. I help early professional women craft a vision of success that aligns with both their goals and their peace.

I often think back to that version of myself, in 2021, who was searching. I took one step, and each decision led to a domino effect. Now, I help others take their next decisive step, navigating transitions. I do this work not from a place of perfection, but from permission: to be present, to move forward, and to rise one decision at a time.

That's the power of making a decision in uncertainty.

It's not about having all the answers. It's about having enough courage to take one step forward. With every step, you start to build momentum. You start to see what once felt hidden in the fog: *You are not lost. You are learning. You are growing. You are becoming.*

You're learning to lead yourself first. When you do that, you don't just survive the pressure; you rise through it. You thrive on the other side of your yes, and in doing so, you make it possible for others to do the same, as I did.

CHAPTER 9

CREATING A CULTURE OF ACCOUNTABILITY AND OWNERSHIP

Angela Hooper-Menifield

Beyond Blame: The Power of Ownership

There's a phrase I often say when coaching leadership teams: Accountability isn't a punishment. It's a promise.

Yet in many organizations, accountability has become synonymous with blame, finger-pointing, or fear. Team members brace for feedback instead of leaning into it. Leaders hesitate to hold others responsible because they don't want to seem harsh or unapproachable. As a result, expectations remain unmet, not because people lack ability, but because they lack clarity, consistency, and connection to outcomes.

> **"ACCOUNTABILITY ISN'T A PUNISHMENT. IT'S A PROMISE."**

Creating a culture of accountability and ownership is about more than enforcing rules or tightening supervision. It's about building an environment where people take pride in their contributions, own their role in outcomes, and feel empowered to speak up, follow through, and deliver results. True accountability is rooted in trust, not control.

When it's done right, something powerful happens:
- Deadlines are respected.
- Challenges are addressed, not hidden.
- Leaders stop chasing, and teams start owning.

In short, accountability becomes cultural, not conditional.

Why Accountability Matters More Than Ever

Today's workplaces are more complex than ever. We're leading across generations, managing hybrid teams, facing economic uncertainty, and navigating rapid change. In that context, accountability can't just be reactive; it has to be built into the fabric of how we lead.

It's the difference between a culture that waits for problems to surface and one that proactively prevents them. It's the difference between employees who comply and those who commit, and between managers who feel like babysitters and leaders who can trust their people to deliver. Here's the truth: Accountability isn't a trait. It's a system. Leaders build that system whether they mean to or not. If you don't define and model what accountability looks like, people will fill in the blanks. That's how miscommunication grows. That's how high performers burn out while others drift. That's how leaders find themselves doing the very work they hired others to do.

When accountability is baked into your leadership philosophy and supported by tools, habits, and language, ownership becomes the norm, not the exception. This chapter will show you how to create that culture, step by step.

It starts with recognizing where the breakdowns happen. Once those have been identified, we rebuild the foundation with clarity, modeling, systems, and empowered conversations. Along the way, I will also show you how you can help your team **Get Their ACT Together™**, not by force, but by alignment, because accountability isn't about control, it's about commitment, capacity, and culture.

Laying the Groundwork: From Expectations to Agreements

Most accountability breakdowns don't start with missed deadlines or poor performance. They start much earlier, with unspoken assumptions disguised as expectations. Leadership isn't just about having high standards. It's about ensuring those standards are shared, understood, and co-owned. That's why one of the most transformative mindset shifts a leader can make is moving from expectations to agreements.

Expectation vs. Agreement: What's the Difference?

- Expectations are often one-sided. They live in the leader's head.
- Agreements are co-created. They live in the shared space between leader and team.
- Expectations say, "I told you what to do."
- Agreements say, "We discussed what success looks like, and you committed to it."

When we operate from expectations, we breed assumptions. When we lead through agreements, we create alignment.

Enter the ACT™ Framework: A Foundation for Accountability

One of the most effective ways I help leaders establish this kind of clarity is by guiding them, and their teams, to Get Their ACT Together™. The ACT™ model is simple, powerful, and actionable:

ACT™	Meaning
A – Alignment	Are we moving in the same direction with shared priorities and goals?
C – Clarity	Are the roles, responsibilities, and deliverables clearly defined?
T – Transparency	Are we being open about progress, blockers, and feedback—early and often?

How ACT™ Creates Cultural Accountability

Alignment ensures everyone is rowing in the same direction. It eliminates competing goals and personal agendas.

Clarity leaves no room for interpretation. When people know exactly what success looks like, they're more confident and consistent in delivering. Transparency builds trust. It creates space for honest updates, proactive problem-solving, and growth without shame.

> "CLARITY LEAVES NO ROOM FOR INTERPRETATION."

When ACT™ becomes a regular part of your leadership rhythm, accountability becomes proactive, not punitive.

How to Use ACT™ in Conversations

Whether you're launching a new project or resetting expectations, use ACT™ as a guide for how you frame conversations:

- "Let's get aligned on what success looks like."
- "How can we clarify who owns what by Friday?"
- "Let's stay transparent about any risks or delays."

It's simple language, but over time, it reshapes behavior.

This is how we begin to move from pressure to partnership; from frustration to follow-through. When your team Gets Their ACT Together™, they don't just perform better, they feel better, because they're no longer guessing. They're leading alongside you.

Manager As Mirror: Modeling Ownership Before Expecting It

When it comes to accountability, leaders often look outward first, at team performance, follow-through, and missed deliverables, but if we want to create a culture of ownership, the mirror must come before the microscope. Culture is shaped more by what leaders model than what they mandate.

- If we want our people to own their role, we must first own ours.
- If we expect clarity from others, we must first communicate clearly.

- If we demand integrity and follow-through, we must become examples of it.

The Accountability Double Standard

Let's be honest: some leaders unintentionally create cultures of low accountability because they haven't been accountable themselves. It's not always about poor intention; sometimes it's about blind spots.

- We cancel one-to-ones because we're "too busy."
- We miss deadlines but expect team members to meet theirs.
- We hold staff to standards we bend ourselves.

When we do this, we send a subtle message that accountability is for them, not for me. The moment we let our leadership status become an excuse instead of a standard, our credibility erodes.

Modeling Accountability Looks Like...

- Admitting when we drop the ball
- Following through on what we said we'd do
- Being on time. Prepared. Present.
- Being willing to be coached or receive feedback
- Owning our role in team dynamics, even the uncomfortable ones

The most powerful phrase a leader can use is, "That's on me." This is not to absorb blame that doesn't belong to you, but to demonstrate ownership in a way that invites your team to do the same.

Personal Reflection: My Leadership Wake-Up Call

There was a moment in my leadership journey when I realized I was holding others accountable for things I hadn't clarified, tracked, or followed up on. I expected excellence, but I hadn't equipped people with the tools or communication needed to deliver it. That realization shifted my approach from monitoring behavior to modeling behavior.

I stopped asking, "Why aren't they getting it done?" and started asking, "What am I doing to make ownership clear and possible?" It changed everything.

Modeling Doesn't Require Perfection, Just Consistency

You don't have to be flawless, but you do have to be transparent and teachable.

When your team sees you:
- Own mistakes
- Clarify expectations
- Ask for feedback
- Stay aligned with your standards

They realize accountability isn't a threat. It's a value.

The Role of Feedback, Follow-Up, and Consequences

You can't build a culture of accountability without feedback. You also can't sustain one without follow-up or consequences.

Even the most well-aligned, clearly communicated teams will drift over time without intentional reinforcement. This is where many leaders drop the ball, not in setting expectations, but in consistently checking back in to ensure they're being met. Accountability is not a one-time conversation. It's a continuous leadership rhythm.

> "ACCOUNTABILITY IS NOT A ONETIME CONVERSATION. IT'S A CONTINUOUS LEADERSHIP RHYTHM."

Feedback: The Oxygen of Accountability

Feedback isn't just about correcting errors; it's about reinforcing alignment.

It must be:

- Frequent (not reserved for annual reviews)
- Focused (connected to shared outcomes)
- Forward-looking (what can be done next time, not just what went wrong)

Examples of feedback that fuel accountability:

- "I noticed we're behind on X. What support do you need?"
- "We agreed to this timeline. Can you walk me through where we are?"
- "You delivered above and beyond my expectations on this. That kind of ownership makes a real impact."

Feedback done well reinforces the behaviors we want more of, not just those we want less of.

Follow-Up: Where Accountability Lives

Question: What is one of the most common leadership gaps?

Answer: Saying something matters, then never asking about it again.

If you:

- Never ask how the project went
- Don't check in on progress
- Or fail to review the result.

...you've unintentionally told your team, "That wasn't important."

Follow-up is how we signal priorities. It also protects performance from drifting into mediocrity. Followup is where follow-through gets measured.

Consequences: Clarity, Not Punishment

Let's be clear: consequences don't have to be punitive. However, they do have to be predictable and proportionate.

In an accountable culture:

- Excellence is recognized
- Patterns of underperformance are addressed
- Expectations aren't adjusted down to fit someone's comfort

Whether it's shifting responsibilities, documenting performance concerns, or limiting new opportunities, there must be clear, fair consequences when agreements aren't kept. Without consequences, accountability is just a suggestion.

A Simple Framework: The Accountability Loop

Use this rhythm to strengthen your accountability culture:

1. Set the agreement – Make expectations mutual and measurable.
2. Check in regularly – Use feedback to assess progress and offer support.
3. Follow up on outcomes – Celebrate what worked. Address what didn't.
4. Adjust or act – Based on what's learned, make changes or apply consequences.
5. Repeat. Consistently. Without emotion, but with intention.

> **"IT'S ONE THING TO GET PEOPLE TO FOLLOW RULES. IT'S ANOTHER TO GET THEM TO TAKE OWNERSHIP."**

This is how accountability becomes normalized, not reactive, but part of the everyday operating system of leadership.

Next, we'll explore how to empower people into ownership instead of enforcing it, and why compliance may get your tasks completed, but commitment creates transformation.

Empowering vs. Policing: Shifting from Compliance to Commitment

It's one thing to get people to follow rules. It's another to get them to take ownership. Many leaders spend valuable time policing behavior, checking in out of fear rather than trust, micromanaging to avoid mistakes, or constantly reminding people of their responsibilities, but accountability fueled by compliance is fragile. It only works when someone's watching. True accountability is built on commitment, the kind that thrives even when no one's looking. Your goal isn't just to enforce accountability. It's to inspire ownership.

The Compliance Trap

When leaders rely too heavily on enforcement, they unknowingly:

- Create dependency instead of initiative
- Discourage autonomy
- Teach people to "just do what they're told"

The result? A team that waits. A team that plays it safe. A team that never grows. That's not leadership. That's supervision. In today's fast-moving environments, you can't scale supervision.

Ownership Grows When People Feel Empowered

Empowerment doesn't mean letting go of standards. It means involving people in defining them.

Ways to foster ownership:

- Invite input when setting goals or timelines
- Assign outcomes, not just tasks
- Ask coaching-style questions instead of giving orders:
  - "What's your plan for tackling this?"
  - "What would success look like?"
  - "Where do you see risks, and how will you manage them?"

These questions shift people from reactive responders to proactive problem-solvers.

Why Empowerment Drives Engagement

According to Gallup's State of the Global Workplace, only 23% of employees are actively engaged, and one of the top factors contributing to disengagement is a lack of autonomy and recognition for contributions.

When people feel like they own their results:

- They show more initiative
- They solve problems faster
- They stick around longer

Ownership is one of the most underutilized engagement tools available to leaders.

Leadership Tools to Move from Policing to Partnering

Try these in your meetings and one-to-ones:

Instead of...	Try this...
"Did you do what I asked?"	"Walk me through how you approached the goal."
"Why wasn't this done on time?"	"What blocked your progress, and how can we prevent that?"
"Next time, let me know sooner."	"What signals could help you raise a flag earlier?"

This approach doesn't weaken standards. It deepens engagement.

The Outcome: Self-Driven Accountability

When accountability is embedded in your team's thinking, not just their to-do list:

- They'll remind you of deadlines.
- They'll ask for help earlier.
- They'll hold themselves to the standard.

> "CULTURE IS BUILT ONE DECISION, ONE CONVERSATION, AND ONLY LEADER AT A TIME."

That's when you know your culture has shifted from compliance to commitment.

In this final section, we'll explore how to apply all of this to build your accountability culture intentionally, starting with where you lead today and scaling it over time.

Building Your Accountability Culture: Start Where You Lead

Creating a culture of accountability and ownership doesn't require a full organizational overhaul or executive mandate. It starts with you. Culture is built one decision, one conversation, and one leader at a time. Whether you manage five people or fifty, you have the power to shape an environment where:

- Ownership is the norm
- Accountability is consistent
- Growth is a shared responsibility

This isn't about perfection. It's about intention and choosing to lead in a way that transforms how others show up.

Start Small. Scale Intentionally.

You don't need to launch a new initiative to begin. Instead, ask:

- Where in my current leadership rhythm can I infuse ACT™ (Alignment, Clarity, Transparency)?
- Which expectations need to be converted into agreements?
- What behaviors do I need to model more consistently?
- Where can I replace reminders with reflection and ownership?

Start with one project, one team member, or one moment of accountability handled better than the last. Small wins build cultural muscle.

Consistency Beats Intensity

Many leaders try to "fix" accountability with one big meeting or a policy update, but what moves the needle is consistency over time:

- Regular check-ins (not just status updates, but growth conversations)
- Celebrating when people own their results, even if the outcome isn't perfect
- Revisiting agreements to keep them current, not just historic
- Ensuring every leader on your team models the same principles

If it's not reinforced, it's not real. Culture is sustained in the follow-through.

Leadership Reflection: Get Your ACT Together™

- Reinforce the ACT™ model by integrating it into your reflection:
- A – Alignment: Is my leadership aligned with what I expect from others?
- C – Clarity: Have I clearly defined what success looks like, for them and me?
- T – Transparency: Am I open about challenges, feedback, and outcomes?

You can't expect what you haven't embodied, and you can't build what you haven't named.

What's Possible When You Lead This Way?

When accountability is normalized:

- Trust deepens
- Performance rises
- Turnover slows
- Leadership stops feeling like babysitting and starts feeling like impact

Your team becomes more than compliant workers; they become committed partners.

Final Charge to the Reader

Accountability and ownership are not "nice-to-haves" for modern leadership; they are non-negotiables, but they don't happen on their own. They happen because you choose to lead differently.

You choose to:
- Model it
- Name it
- Reinforce it
- Celebrate it
- Expect it without apology

When you lead with ownership, you don't just get better results, you build better leaders.

CHAPTER 10

LEADING ACROSS DIFFERENCES:

EQUITY, EMPATHY, AND EVERYDAY CHOICES

Amber Reneé Letbetter

Noticing the Difference

April 2009.

My classmates and I were preparing for the Spring PTA meeting, where we would showcase the artwork we'd been creating since the beginning of the semester. We were proud seventh graders, eager to brag and show our parents what we had accomplished. I was one of two Black girls in my art class at a predominantly white middle school. By this point in my education, this was usually the case, so navigating white spaces felt routine, so I thought.

As our parents arrived, we eagerly showed our paintings, pottery, drawings, and digital prints, explaining in great detail who our muses were and why we chose our particular subjects. Throughout the night, parents kept noting how "articulate" and "well spoken" they thought I was.

"Oh my goodness, you speak so well."

"Wow! You are so eloquent."

In a vacuum, these comments might seem complimentary. I was, in fact, well spoken and quite eloquent, but so were my white peers. We had the same teachers, read the same books, completed the same homework, and used similar vocabulary. Yet, the overwhelming shock and awe were directed only at me. I couldn't help but feel it was because their expectations of how a young Black girl would speak didn't align with my reality.

They expected expressive, silver-tongued speech from the white children, but not from me. I didn't feel empowered. I felt small, judged. It was weird. Ironically, I couldn't find the words to explain why I was uncomfortable.

I even tried to gaslight myself into believing I was overreacting. These parents didn't mean any harm; how could they? They were simply complimenting me, right? Maybe they were conflating charisma with eloquence? But why did I feel so yucky about it? Why didn't I feel praised?

Though I'm now twenty-nine, that moment still sits with me. I think about it more than I ever expected to at thirteen. I've since realized those "compliments" were microaggressions, subtle, unintentional forms of prejudice that manifested as backhanded praise. I wish I had that understanding in my toolbox back then. If I had, I likely wouldn't have spent sleepless nights wondering what they meant. I would have felt empowered to name it in real time. I wouldn't have shrank in the room, questioning why I was being singled out for simply existing the same way my white classmates did.

Ironically, that night is where my leadership journey began. I was determined that no other student would feel the way I did: small, lonely, misunderstood, or "othered." I now know, without a doubt, that Diversity, Equity, and Inclusion (DEI) is paramount in all spaces.

Reframing DEI for a New Generation

In today's world and political climate, DEI has unfortunately become a negative buzzword. It has been distorted into something it was never intended to be. DEI is not about corporate quotas or tax breaks. It's about creating spaces where people, no matter their background, are seen and heard. It's about leading people as they are.

Diversity allows us to learn and grow from everyone's uniqueness, making us stronger, more adaptable, and better equipped to face challenges. Inclusion isn't something you "do"; it's how you are. It is a universal human right and involves providing equal access, opportunities, and eliminating discrimination. It requires awareness of unconscious biases and a willingness to manage them.

"INCLUSION ISN'T SOMETHING YOU DO; IT'S HOW YOU ARE."

Equity is not the same as equality. It means understanding what each person uniquely needs to thrive. Our differences can create barriers, so we must ensure equity before we can expect equality.

Due to the vilification of DEI in some circles, I propose a reframing: EEE: Equity, Empathy, and Everyday Choices.

- Equity: Fairness in opportunity, not sameness in treatment.
- Empathy: Listening, learning, and leading with understanding.
- Everyday Choices: The micro-decisions we make daily that collectively shape our organizational culture.

Micro-decisions may seem insignificant alone, but together, they determine how inclusive or exclusive a space becomes. Ask yourself: How can implementing EEE impact your leadership style?

The Leadership Lens: Inclusion in Action

Let's put this new EEE framework to the test. How does inclusion show up in our micro-decisions as leaders?

Who Gets Invited to Speak or Lead?

As leaders, we often choose who to empower. Inclusive leaders ensure opportunities are distributed equitably, not just to the most familiar or vocal individuals. We can actively seek input from underrepresented voices, encourage diverse perspectives, and ensure visibility at all levels. A simple decision like choosing who gets the mic can shape long-term equity.

How Is Feedback Given?

"INCLUSIVE LEADERS GIVE FEEDBACK RESPECTFULLY, EQUITABLY, AND WITH CULTURAL AWARENESS."

Inclusive leaders give feedback respectfully, equitably, and with cultural awareness. Feedback should be tailored to individual communication styles, offered as part of a dialogue, not a directive, and checked for bias. Inclusive feedback makes it clear that everyone's growth matters.

How Are Policies Applied?

Policies should be applied with nuance, not rigidity. Inclusive leaders balance consistency with empathy. Flexibility in schedules, communication methods, or resources can uphold equity while avoiding favoritism. This shows that people are seen as individuals.

Whose Voices Are Heard in Meetings?

Inclusive leaders create space for quieter team members, avoid interruptions, and ensure balanced participation. Tools like rotating facilitators or structured turn-taking elevate diverse voices and build psychological safety. Inclusion isn't a department. It's a daily decision.

Inclusive Leadership As a Framework

To support inclusive leadership, use the **SEE™** Framework:

- **S – Stop and Check Your Bias:** Pause and reflect before making decisions. Ask, "Am I being objective?" or "Whose perspective is missing?" This builds equity and trust.
- **E – Engage with Curiosity:** Listen actively and ask thoughtful questions. Understand the "why" behind others' perspectives. This fosters psychological safety and connection.
- **E – Elevate Voices Not Usually Heard:** Intentionally amplify voices that are often overlooked. Rotate leadership roles, validate contributions, and invite input from all levels.

Next time you make a micro-decision, take a moment to ensure you're SEEing how your leadership affects your team.

Success Story: How Inclusive Leadership Transformed a Product Launch

(All names and organizations are fictional. Any resemblance to real persons or entities is purely coincidental.)

Reprogramming your leadership style for inclusion can feel overwhelming, but real-world examples show how powerful it can be. At a mid-sized tech company called Hooper Technology, the product team was preparing to launch a new app for remote workers. The team was skilled but lacked diversity in background and thought. Leadership often relied on a small group of senior developers, which led to products that were overly technical and inaccessible.

Enter Ameir, a newly promoted product manager known for her inclusive leadership. From day one, she prioritized inclusion. She rotated facilitators, accepted anonymous ideas, and encouraged respectful participation from everyone.

During one design review, a junior designer, Audrey, raised concerns about accessibility for visually impaired users. In the past, her insights had been brushed aside, but under Ameir's leadership, her input was not only heard, it was explored. Ameir asked, "How might we ensure this feature works for all users?" and encouraged testing with assistive technologies.

This moment marked a shift. The team began engaging with greater curiosity and empathy. They expanded their user testing pool to include people with disabilities, older users, and individuals from non-technical backgrounds. A bilingual customer support representative, Terry, was invited to a design sprint, where he pointed out cultural and language nuances that could impact how global users interacted with the app. His suggestions led to the integration of more inclusive language and customizable interface options.

Ameir also encouraged the team to "stop and check their bias" before making design or development decisions. For example, when someone assumed users would be tech-savvy or have high-speed internet, Ameir prompted the team to consider lower-bandwidth environments and varied digital literacy levels.

The result? The final product was significantly more user-friendly, accessible, and widely applicable than previous iterations. The app launch exceeded expectations: user adoption was 35% higher in international markets, customer satisfaction scores rose by 20%, and the app received positive press for its inclusive design. Internally, employee engagement also improved as team members reported feeling more respected, heard, and motivated.

Most importantly, Ameir's leadership style began to influence other departments. Leaders across Hooper Technology started adopting similar inclusive practices, inviting diverse perspectives, applying policies with empathy, and creating space for all voices to contribute meaningfully. In the end, inclusive leadership didn't just change a product; it transformed a culture. By elevating unheard voices, SEEing the contribution of others, engaging with curiosity, and making space for difference, Ameir helped unlock innovation and foster a more equitable and successful workplace.

A Call to Conscious Leadership

In today's increasingly diverse and interconnected world, inclusive leadership is not just a moral imperative; it's also a business and cultural advantage. At the heart of inclusive leadership lie four powerful principles: empathy, equity, micro-decisions, and inclusion. Together, these create a foundation for leading in ways that bring out the best in individuals and teams.

> **"EMPATHETIC LEADERS CREATE PSYCHOLOGICALLY SAFE SPACES WHERE INDIVIDUALS FEEL SEEN, VALUED, AND RESPECTED."**

Empathy allows leaders to connect with people beyond roles or responsibilities. It means actively listening, seeking to understand others' experiences, and responding with compassion rather than assumption. Empathetic leaders create psychologically safe spaces where individuals feel seen, valued, and respected. This human connection drives trust, engagement, and retention, key ingredients for any thriving organization.

Equity goes a step further, recognizing that not everyone starts from the same place or faces the same barriers. While equality treats everyone the same, equity adjusts to individual needs to create fairness in access, support, and opportunity. Inclusive leaders apply equity in how they assign work, evaluate performance, and offer growth opportunities. They understand that fair treatment means recognizing and addressing systemic imbalances, both big and small.

This brings us to the micro-decisions, the countless small choices leaders make every day, often without realizing their impact. Who gets invited to speak in meetings? Whose ideas are validated? Who receives feedback, and how? These decisions may seem minor in the moment, but collectively, they shape culture, signal value, and determine who thrives. Inclusive leaders pause to check their biases, ask "Whose voice is missing?" and lead with intentionality. Through consistent, inclusive micro-decisions, they build a workplace where everyone has the chance to grow, contribute, and lead.

Inclusion is the outcome of putting empathy, equity, and thoughtful decision-making into practice. It's about more than having diverse representation; it's about creating a culture where all people feel they belong and can fully participate. Inclusive leaders are proactive: they elevate voices not usually heard, adapt policies with nuance, and lead with curiosity rather than judgment. They foster innovation by drawing on the full range of perspectives within their teams, and they strengthen resilience by ensuring no one is left out or left behind.

> **"INCLUSION IS THE OUTCOME OF PUTTING EMPATHY, EQUITY, AND THOUGHTFUL DECISION-MAKING INTO PRACTICE."**

Inclusive leadership is not a one-time effort or a checklist; it's a daily commitment. It shows up in tone, timing, and behavior. It's practiced in how leaders give feedback, recognize contributions, and respond to challenges. When done consistently, it transforms workplaces into environments where people are not only included but also empowered.

In a world that demands adaptability, empathy, and collaboration, inclusive leadership is not just the right thing to do; it's the smart thing to do. It fuels performance, deepens connection, and ensures every voice has a place and purpose. By leading with empathy, applying equity, making thoughtful micro-decisions, and centering inclusion, leaders can create a lasting impact for individuals, teams, and organizations as a whole.

You don't have to be a DEI expert or even an EEE expert. You just have to care and, most importantly, ACT.

III

Transformational
Leadership & Legacy

*G*reat leadership doesn't end with results; it extends to people, purpose, and legacy. This final section invites you to think beyond today's to-do list and explore the long game of leadership. It's about transformation: your own and the transformation you create for others.

Whether you're managing burnout, preparing future leaders, or refining your conflict skills, these chapters will challenge you to lead with foresight and finish well. Ultimately, leadership isn't just about what you build; it's about what you leave behind.

As you read these closing chapters, ask yourself: What will your leadership echo long after the work is done?

CHAPTER 11

FROM BOSS TO VISIONARY:

TRANSFORM YOUR MANAGEMENT STYLE INTO REAL LEADERSHIP

Sharon Eason

When Being the Boss Isn't Enough

In the early stages of building my business, being the boss worked. I wore every hat, accountant, marketer, and project manager, and prided myself on being the go-to for everything. Clients loved the personal attention, and team members saw me as the final word. That kind of hands-on leadership earned me praise and built momentum, but over time, what once felt empowering began to feel burdensome.

The truth is, when you're operating as the sole engine of progress, you leave no room for others to lead. Decision bottlenecks, innovation stalls, and burnout creeps in quietly, but steadily. There was a time when I thought I was doing everything right. I had the title, the credentials, and the respect of my team. I ran a tight ship, made the decisions, kept the wheels turning, and everyone knew I was in charge.

> "WHEN YOU'RE OPERATING AS THE SOLE ENGINE OF PROGRESS, YOU LEAVE NO ROOM FOR OTHERS TO LEAD."

But quietly, something was not working. I was managing tasks, putting out fires, and solving problems, yet it felt like I was carrying the weight of the business alone. My team was doing what I asked, but not much more. I was the engine, the driver, the fuel, and truthfully, I was running on fumes.

That's when it hit me: I wasn't leading. I was just bossing. It's easy to fall into the trap of equating management with leadership. After all, we're taught to manage people, systems, time, and outcomes, but management alone doesn't move people. It doesn't inspire growth. It certainly doesn't build a legacy.

Leadership is different. It's not about doing more. It's about doing what matters. It's about creating clarity, casting vision, and trusting others to step up, even if that means stepping back. When I finally admitted to myself that being "the boss" wasn't enough, everything began to shift. Not overnight, but slowly, and powerfully. I started asking different questions, not just of my team, but of myself.

> "LEADERSHIP...IS NOT ABOUT DOING MORE. IT'S ABOUT DOING WHAT MATTERS."

That was the beginning of my transformation: from the boss holding it all together... to the visionary building something that could stand on its own.

The Difference Between Management and Leadership

There is a subtle but powerful difference between managing and leading. When you're in the thick of running a business or organization, it's easy to blur the lines between the two. Management is about maintenance. Leadership is about movement.

Managers ensure things get done. They create order, structure, and systems. They are excellent at solving problems, monitoring performance, and making sure everyone stays on task. There's nothing wrong with that. It's essential, but management alone will not drive growth or ignite transformation.

Leadership, on the other hand, is visionary. Leaders are future-focused. They think in terms of impact and possibility, not just productivity. They create space for innovation and growth, and they empower others to own outcomes, not just complete checklists.

> **"LEADERSHIP IS VISIONARY. LEADERS ARE FUTURE-FOCUSED."**

Here's how I've come to understand the two:

Managers	Visionary Leaders
Direct people	Inspire people
Prioritize efficiency	Prioritize alignment and purpose
Focus on tasks and timelines	Focus on outcomes and evolution
Seek compliance	Cultivate commitment
Delegate responsibility	Share ownership and trust
Control processes	Empower people

Looking back, I was managing more than I was leading. I was efficient and dependable, but I wasn't painting a vision my team could rally behind. Without that vision, everyone defaulted to doing what was required, not what was possible.

The shift began when I stopped asking, "What needs to get done?" and started asking, "Where are we going, and who do we need to become to get there?"

That single question pulled me out of manager mode and into my true role as a leader. I remember one specific moment when I caught myself defaulting to management. A team member was struggling to complete a client report, and instead of guiding her through it, I jumped in, fixed the formatting, rewrote the summary, and sent it off.

At the time, I told myself it was just faster to do it myself, but afterward, I realized two things: she did not grow from that experience, and I had reinforced a pattern of dependency. That moment stuck with me. Now, in a similar situation, I would coach her through the process, help her see the standard we're aiming for, and empower her to revise and own the work.

That is the difference between managing the task and leading the person.

My Turning Point: From Control to Clarity

My turning point did not come from a dramatic breakdown, walkout, or financial collapse. It came from exhaustion and a quiet, persistent inner knowing: This is not sustainable.

I remember sitting in my office one evening, long after everyone had gone home. The lights were off, and I was staring at my laptop, not working, just thinking. I realized I was exhausted not from the work itself, but from holding it all alone. In that silence, it hit me: I could not scale a vision I had not shared. That night, I made the quiet decision to stop managing by control and start leading by clarity.

I was doing it all, reviewing every detail, double-checking every decision, filling every gap. My team was capable, but I had not given them the space or the structure to lead. I thought I was protecting the business. In reality, I was bottlenecking its growth.

At the heart of it, I was clinging to control because I was afraid of what might happen if I let go. Would they drop the ball? Would clients notice? Would I be seen as less competent if I weren't hands-on with every moving part?

But here's what I realized: control isn't the same as clarity. Control creates dependency. Clarity creates ownership. So, I made a conscious decision to shift from controlling every outcome to getting clear on the outcomes that mattered most. That meant:

- Defining a clear vision and purpose for the business.
- Articulating roles, expectations, and values with precision.
- Letting my team make decisions and trusting them to learn through doing.
- Creating systems that supported accountability without my constant input.

Letting go wasn't easy, but it was liberating. The more clarity I gave my team, the more confident they became. They didn't need micromanagement; they needed direction and trust.

That's when I began to see my leadership evolve. I wasn't just managing processes, I was developing people. I was growing a culture of ownership. I was finally stepping into the role I was meant to play: VISIONARY.

The Cost of Staying the Boss

Staying in boss mode might feel comfortable. It's familiar, it's efficient, and it gives you control, but the long-term cost is steep:

- Growth stalls because everything depends on your bandwidth.
- Team disengagement rises because people are not trusted to lead.
- You become the bottleneck, the single point of failure in your business.
- Burnout becomes inevitable because you are carrying the load for everyone.

Let me give you a real-life example. I once worked with a business owner named Dana, who ran a successful creative agency. She was passionate, hands-on, and committed to excellence, but she reviewed every proposal, approved every graphic, and answered every client email. Her team felt underutilized and untrusted. She missed out on business development opportunities simply because there was no capacity left in her day.

Eventually, she hit a wall. One day, a high-value client churned, and she hadn't even seen it coming. Not because the team didn't care, but because they'd stopped offering insights she never asked for. They assumed she wanted control, not collaboration.

If any of these signs sound familiar, know this: the problem isn't you; it's the model. The good news is, there's a better way.

Visionary Leadership in Action

Visionary leadership isn't about charisma or corner offices. It's about intentionality. It's about shifting from running everything to aligning everything, people, strategy, and culture, toward a shared vision.

Once I decided to stop clinging to control and start leading with purpose, I began developing what I now call the **Visionary Leadership Framework™**, a model rooted in clarity, culture, strategic delegation, and legacy thinking. These weren't things I read in a book. They were forged through experience, reflection, and a lot of real-world trial and error.

> "VISIONARY LEADERSHIP ISN'T ABOUT CHARISMA ... IT'S ABOUT INTENTIONALITY."

Pillar 1: Clarity of Vision

A visionary knows where they're going and why. Once I articulated my business's deeper purpose, to empower clients through financial clarity and confidence, it became easier to make decisions, set priorities, and rally my team. We weren't just offering services. We were changing outcomes.

Every project, every conversation began to connect back to that vision. For example, during a year of economic uncertainty, I led a strategy meeting where I re-

147

minded the team: "Our mission isn't just taxes and books. It's helping small business owners sleep at night." That reset helped us stay focused on serving proactively, not just reactively.

Pillar 2: Empowered Team Culture

Visionary leaders do not hoard power; they distribute it. I stopped solving every problem myself. Instead, I started asking better questions. I encouraged my team to bring solutions, not just challenges. I invested in their growth, invited them to share their perspectives, and made space for them to lead within their roles.

> **"VISIONARY LEADERS DO NOT HOARD POWER; THEY DISTRIBUTE IT."**

One team member, initially quiet in meetings, began leading our monthly financial deep dives after being encouraged to present her analysis. Not only did it build her confidence, but it also improved how we caught financial anomalies earlier. Her ownership created a ripple effect that raised the standard across the entire team.

Pillar 3: Strategic Delegation

Letting go is tough, but it's necessary to move forward. Delegation is more than offloading tasks; it's about releasing the right responsibilities to the right people so you can focus on vision and growth. Once I understood this, I built systems that allowed my team to operate independently, while keeping me informed, but not involved in every detail.

For instance, I created a weekly briefing format that allowed department leads to share progress, metrics, and blockers. That simple structure saved me hours while giving them the framework to operate like mini-CEOs within their domains.

Pillar 4: Legacy Thinking

Visionaries don't lead for today, they build for tomorrow. Every time I made a decision, I started asking: "Does this move us closer to where we want to be long-term?" That lens changed everything, from the way I hired to the services I offered to the boundaries I set.

> **"VISIONARIES DON'T LEAD FOR TODAY, THEY BUILD FOR TOMORROW."**

We began documenting processes not just for efficiency, but for continuity. I trained my team to think about scalability, sustainability, and succession. That forward-thinking culture took root and started shaping decisions at every level.

Legacy is not about ego. It's about impact. It's about creating something that continues to serve, even when you're no longer at the center of it.

These four pillars became the backbone of my new leadership style. I wasn't managing tasks anymore. I was nurturing momentum.

Stepping into visionary leadership requires more than just adopting new frameworks. It required a fundamental internal shift. The next stage of my journey wasn't about what I was building; it was about what I was willing to release. That realization led me into the next critical phase of my transformation: learning how to truly let go so that my business and my leadership could level up.

Letting Go to Level Up

Adopting visionary leadership didn't happen because I suddenly had more time, more help, or more resources. It happened because I decided to lead differently. To step into that next level, I had to confront one of the hardest truths of all: I was in my way.

Letting go is not a passive process. It's a leadership discipline that demands trust, intention, and courage. Many of us hold on tightly, not because we don't believe in others, but because we're afraid of losing control, standards, or our relevance. Ironically, the tighter we grip, the more we suffocate the very growth we're hoping to create.

"IF EVERYTHING FLOWS THROUGH YOU, NOTHING CAN SCALE BEYOND YOU."

When you've built something from the ground up, every client relationship, every process, every detail, it's tempting to believe that your involvement is the glue holding it all together. In some ways, that is true, but the reality is that mindset quickly becomes a ceiling. If everything flows through you, nothing can scale beyond you.

So, what does letting go look like in practice?

- Start with trust, not perfection. Give your team room to grow. Accept that mistakes will happen and use them as opportunities to coach, not correct.

- Document and delegate with clarity. I created SOPs (Standard Operating Procedures) not just for efficiency, but to provide my team with confidence and consistency. Delegation does not mean dumping; it means transferring authority along with the tools and training to succeed.

- Empower through accountability. I shifted from asking, "Did you get it done?" to "What was your process and what did you learn?" This created a culture where people took ownership of outcomes, not just assignments.
- Step back strategically. I gave up tasks that didn't require my unique insight so I could invest in what only I could do, relationship building and strategic growth.

One powerful example came when I handed over client onboarding to my operations lead. Initially, I was nervous. I had always done it myself and knew the nuances well, but once we co-created a workflow, trained her thoroughly, and let her run with it, she exceeded expectations. She streamlined the process and elevated the client's experience with thoughtful touches I hadn't even considered.

That experience reinforced something critical: letting go does not mean quality drops. It often means it gets better. Letting go did not mean abandoning excellence. It meant creating conditions where excellence could thrive without my constant supervision. That required:

- Documented systems so team members had structure without needing to ask.
- Trust, even when mistakes were made (because they were part of the learning process).
- Clear boundaries around my own time, so I

could work *on the business instead of being buried in it.*

Most importantly, it required me to shift my identity from the problem-solver and chief operator to the visionary steward of something bigger than myself.

"LETTING GO DID NOT DIMINISH MY ROLE. IT REDEFINED IT."

What happened next surprised me. My team stepped up. Clients noticed the increased efficiency and responsiveness. We stopped reacting and started proactively growing, not just in revenue, but in reputation, impact, and confidence. Letting go did not diminish my role. It redefined it, and gave my business room to breathe, evolve, and thrive in ways I couldn't have imagined when I was stuck trying to do it all myself.

The Results: Real Leadership in Motion

Leadership is not about titles or control; it's about transformation. Once I embraced this shift fully, the impact started to show up everywhere: in how I worked, how my team showed up, and how my clients experienced our service.

The transformation was not instant, but it was undeniable. My team no longer waited to be told what to do. They anticipated needs. They created new solutions. They contributed fresh, strategic ideas and took initiative in ways I once only hoped for. What used to feel like a team of doers became a team of thinkers, strategic, empowered, and invested.

One tangible example came when we implemented a quarterly leadership roundtable. Each department leader was invited to present not just updates, but proposals to improve client service, tighten internal processes, or introduce new tools. During one meeting, our client services manager suggested automating the onboarding workflow using a CRM integration. We implemented her idea, and it cut onboarding time by 40%.

That's visionary leadership in motion, not because I made the decision, but because I created the environment where someone else could.

Our clients began to notice, too. They no longer saw us as simply a service provider; we became trusted advisors. They commented on how prepared, proactive, and communicative the team was, evidence of the deeper ownership culture we had built behind the scenes.

I also began receiving more speaking invitations, partnership opportunities, and referrals, because leadership that is visible, consistent, and visionary attracts momentum.

Here are a few resources that helped reinforce our transformation:

- *Dare to Lead* by Brené Brown – reminded me that vulnerability, trust, and courage are the foundation of real leadership.
- *Leaders Eat Last by Simon Sinek – emphasized that great leaders prioritize people, fostering safety and trust within teams.*
- *Drive* by Daniel H. Pink – unpacked the psychology of motivation and how autonomy, mastery, and purpose fuel engagement.

- *The 5 Levels of Leadership* by John C. Maxwell – outlined a roadmap for growing influence beyond authority.
- *Essentialism* by Greg McKeown – helped me focus on what matters and eliminate the noise that distracts from visionary thinking.
- *Radical Candor* by Kim Scott – taught me how to challenge directly while still caring personally, a powerful balance for developing others.

The biggest result, though, wasn't external; it was internal. I began to lead from a place of peace instead of pressure. I felt aligned, empowered, and energized. That inner shift influenced everything else around me.

Visionary leadership, I realized, wasn't about changing others. It was about changing how I show up and trusting that the ripple effect would follow, and it did.

Becoming the Leader You Were Meant to Be

Visionary leadership is not the end of the journey; it's the beginning of leading with legacy in mind. Once you've experienced the clarity, collaboration, and momentum that come from stepping into true leadership, you'll never want to go back to managing by default. You'll start to see leadership not as a role, but as a responsibility to inspire transformation in others.

This transformation begins with you, but it doesn't end there. It ripples into your team, your clients, your community, and eventually into your legacy.

I invite you to pause here, not just to reflect on what you've read, but to act on what has stirred inside of you.

Ask yourself:

- Where am I managing when I could be leading?
- What vision am I truly casting, and does my team feel connected to it?
- What do I need to release to fully step into visionary leadership?

Start small if you need to. Delegate one thing. Recast your mission in a team meeting. Listen more than you speak. Share your vision out loud. Let someone else shine, and celebrate their win.

This is how real leadership takes shape. When you lead with vision, you don't just move projects forward, you move people. You don't just grow a business; you grow a movement. You don't just create results; you create resonance.

That is the power of shifting from boss to visionary. It's not about what you can control; it's about what you're willing to build through others, with courage, clarity, and compassion. That is where your legacy begins. Because when your leadership becomes legacy, you don't just change your business, you elevate and expand the possibilities for everyone who walks with you.

CHAPTER 12

THE ART OF DIFFICULT CONVERSATIONS:

LEADING THROUGH CONFLICT

Dr. Katherine Y. Baines Brown

*L*eading requires confronting the tensions within, between, and around us. In many instances, leadership is often celebrated in terms of vision, charisma, and decisiveness, but in my experience, the real proving ground for leadership lies in the quiet tension before a difficult conversation. It is in that pause, where truth and discomfort meet, that leadership is either deepened or diminished.

Over the years, I've worn many hats: professor, national CPR spokesperson, founder, mother,

> **"NOT ALL CONFLICT IS LOUD."**

survivor, but one of the most quietly shaping roles I hold is as the founder of the KYB Leadership Academy. We've worked with over 30 cohorts across the world, mentoring students in self-esteem, social-emotional learning, leadership, and teaching them advocacy. With each new group, I was reminded that leadership is less about managing others and more about stewarding truth with grace. Truth, when fully embraced, invites conflict.

Not all conflict is loud. Some conflict shows up as resistance, and other conflict as silence. Some conflict presents as the tightening in your chest when you know you need to say something that may change everything.

The Layers of Conflict

Too often, we frame conflict as something external: a disagreement between two people, a confrontation waiting to be avoided or won, but real leadership demands a broader lens.

- There are conflicts that happen within ourselves: the tug-of-war between fear and courage, imposter syndrome and confidence, silence and voice.
- There are conflicts within others: moments when people are not fighting us, but their pain, limitations, or storylines.
- There are systemic conflicts: cultural norms, injustices, or generational patterns that make growth harder than it should be.
- There are interpersonal conflicts: the kind where someone lashes out, resists correction, or says the expectations are too high.
- There are also relational conflicts, where the desire to be liked as a speaker or educator comes into tension with the responsibility to lead and correct.

In leadership, all of these exist, sometimes at once. The art of difficult conversations is learning how to name, hold, and move through them without letting go of the humanity in yourself or others.

My Discomfort with Truth

When I started KYB Leadership Academy, I had a

vision for developing youth leaders from underserved communities. What I didn't expect was how uncomfortable I would feel giving them feedback.

Many of the students were learning life skills, how to write an email, introduce themselves in a room, or lead a group, for the first time. I found myself hesitating. "What if I discourage them?" "What if they think I'm judging them?" I wanted to lead with encouragement, not criticism.

But then I realized that avoiding the truth is not love. To develop leaders, I had to get over my discomfort with tension. I had to learn how to say:

- "That wasn't clear. Let's go back and revise it."
- "You're not showing up prepared. Why is that?"
- "You have potential, but you're not leading yet. Let's give you an opportunity to lead."

Each conversation required me to lead through conflict, not avoid it. The more I engaged with truth, the more I saw growth. One student told me, "No one ever told me I could lead, but when you corrected me, I believed you saw more in me." That stayed with me. Correction without care is criticism, but correction with compassion is coaching.

Conflict as Leadership Development

When students are trying to lead, they will face their inner conflict: "Am I good enough? Will they follow me? What if I fail?"

Some college students struggled with behaviors that high school students who had greater exposure had already mastered. I had to teach the simple act of saying "good morning" or showing up on time. That too was conflict, conflict with professional norms, personal habits, and sometimes generational differences.

There were moments when students resisted the structure, lashed out, or called the program "too hard." Those moments hurt. I carried those wounds privately, knowing I was pouring into them even when they didn't see it yet.

But here's what happened years later: those same students came back and said, "Dr. Katherine, thank you. We needed that. You didn't need to change; we needed to grow."

For a while, I softened my approach out of fear of not being liked, but their return reminded me: rigor with love is not the enemy, it's the path. I returned to my standard. I stayed true to my calling. I served from the heart, with clear expectations and consistency for every cohort. Leadership is not about popularity; it's about transformation.

Tools That Help

Difficult conversations don't get easier, but you get better at preparing for them. Here are a few tools I use:

- Ask for permission: "May I offer you some feedback?"
- Lead with care: "Here's what I noticed, and I want to help you grow."
- Clarify your intent: "This is not a judgment. It's an opportunity."
- Make space for response: "How did that land for you?"

Sometimes, leadership means slowing down to let someone else catch up. Other times, it means speeding up to challenge someone to rise.

The Mirror Matters Too

It's easy to become the person who gives feedback, but a true leader must also be willing to receive it. I remember when a young facilitator on my team pulled me aside. "Dr. Brown," she said gently, "I know your standard is high, but some of the students feel like they can't make a mistake."

That was hard to hear, but she wasn't wrong. My fear of them being unprepared had made me too rigid. I took her feedback to heart. In the next session, I led with more empathy. I started by sharing a time I failed as a speaker. That small shift opened the room. We cannot demand humility from others when we're unwilling to demonstrate humility ourselves.

Leading in a Tense World

In the broader world, we see conflict everywhere, political division, social unrest, and cultural misunderstandings. As leaders, we are called to be bridges in broken places, but that begins in small rooms, with personal conversations, and a willingness to say, "I see more in you than you see right now."

> "AS LEADERS, WE ARE CALLED TO BE BRIDGES IN BROKEN PLACES."

Difficult conversations can change the trajectory of someone's life when handled well, but they must be practiced, modeled, and revisited with love. Leadership means having clear communication, clear expectations, and clarity of vision. We must always A.I.M. for success: Authenticity, Integrity, and Mission, without losing what makes our leadership effective.

Conclusion: The Work and the Gift

The more I led through conflict, the more I learned that we don't serve people by sparing them discomfort. We serve them by walking with them through it. Whether you're teaching a teen how to lead, guiding a team toward excellence, or facing your reflection after a misstep, leadership requires courage to speak, courage to listen, and courage to stay in the room when things get hard. Most of all, leadership requires courage to believe that the other side of conflict isn't separation, it's transformation. That's the real art, and it is worth mastering.

CHAPTER 13

SUSTAINABLE LEADERSHIP:

AVOIDING BURNOUT AND CULTIVATING GROWTH

Olive Cyrus

I want to start this chapter with a quote about leadership:

"A leader is one who knows the way, goes the way, and shows the way." – John C. Maxwell

The big question is: What do you want most in your career? This chapter reflects my leadership evolution, shaped by decades of military and civilian healthcare leadership, where I have learned that burnout and brilliance often coexist, but they don't have to. I navigated the roadmap of sustainable leadership and began viewing obstacles as opportunities to learn and cultivate growth. I call it developing resilience.

In today's fast-paced world, leadership is often synonymous with constant motion, decision-making, problem-solving, and the ever-present pressure to perform. While ambition and drive fuel progress, the relentless pursuit of excellence can come at a cost: burnout, disconnection, and unsustainable practices that undermine both personal well-being and organizational health.

Sustainable Leadership

Sustainable leadership offers a new path, one that

prioritizes balance, purpose, and resilience. It's about leading with intention, nurturing growth without sacrificing health, and creating environments where people can thrive, not just survive.

This path begins with self-awareness and the courage to redefine what success means. It involves cultivating habits that support mental, emotional, and physical well-being, while also fostering collaboration, innovation, and long-term impact.

Sustainable leaders are not only effective, they are enduring. They know when to push forward and when to pause. They lead from within, guided by values, empathy, and a commitment to continuous growth for themselves and those around them.

"SUSTAINABLE LEADERS ARE NOT ONLY EFFECTIVE, THEY ARE ENDURING."

In this chapter, I will share practical strategies to prevent burnout, promote mindful leadership, and establish a foundation for growth that is both powerful and sustainable, a foundation that transitions from burnout to balance, from pressure to purpose.

My Leadership Journey

With over 36 years of nursing experience, my leadership journey began early in my career as an active-duty officer in the Air Force. I served in the Nurse Corps with certifications in medical-surgical and ambulatory care, and received intensive training as a flight nurse aboard C-17 aircraft. In addition, I have successfully completed 27 years of federal service, across private and federal sectors, culminating in my role as Chief Nurse at the VA.

Each step expanded my understanding of what leadership demands and what it costs when you're not supported. I was known to be a fast burner, quickly rising through the ranks. I worked hard and produced excellent results. My interest in leadership grew deeper, leading me to earn a doctor of nursing degree with an emphasis in leadership from Duke University.

Working in all these segments of healthcare provided numerous leadership opportunities, some well-orchestrated, others lacking direction. To truly understand leadership from novice to experienced, I had to ask myself: Does burnout hinder your true leadership experience?

Don't get me wrong, I've had many rewarding leadership roles. Not all of them led to burnout, but a few certainly did. My "get-it-done" attitude often led to exhaustion. Leadership and burnout don't necessarily go hand in hand, but they're often connected.

According to the Harvard Business Review (May 18, 2023): More than 50% of managers report feeling burned out, a number slightly higher than that of employees more broadly. The causes include the challenges of the pandemic, combined with the experience of three hallmarks of burnout: exhaustion, cynicism, and a perceived lack of professional accomplishment.

The burnout I experienced stemmed largely from not having the right tools to sustain leadership growth or manage burnout effectively. There's a fallacy that high achievers automatically have the skills they need simply because they perform at a high level.

I often didn't speak up for help as I saw it as a weakness. I frequently found myself feeling defeated, lost, and filled with anxiety. I began to question my skills as a leader. Was I setting my goals too high? On top of that, I began questioning how I could cultivate growth in my leadership team and among the people I supervise.

Many of my roles carried tremendous responsibility, from ensuring facility accreditation to overseeing the training, education, and mentorship of nurses.

Eventually, continuing to support both staff and the organization began to feel burdensome. Asking questions and receiving feedback from colleagues and staff became increasingly rare. You may be wondering: What did I do about it?

As you continue reading, you'll find tips, books, and other methods I used to cultivate sustainable leadership. My new journey was enhanced by getting a coach, reading leadership books, listening to podcasts, and joining the John C. Maxwell Team.

What I needed was a reset, an uplift to develop a new vision for myself. I've observed managers and read many published articles on burnout. I realized that this wasn't a journey I could take alone.

Many managers are feeling burned out. Middle managers, in particular, often feel the pressure of executing strategy from above while coaching and developing their teams below, frequently without receiving the same level of development or empowerment from senior leadership. I often roll up my sleeves to work alongside my teams, especially given the increased turnover rates in recent years.

In the roles where I felt I did a fantastic job as a leader and didn't suffer from burnout, team building, and mentoring were at the forefront. This was essential in helping me, as a new leader, become a trailblazer. Small on-the-job workshops and leadership training programs, such as the Health Care Leadership and Development Program, were available to Veterans Administration employees who aspired to leadership roles. This one-year interactive immersion was led by seasoned, top-notch leaders who shared their experiences and tips for navigating such a role. During these informative sessions, even with well-experienced leaders, I still observed the underlying burn-out that some of them faced.

I began to immerse myself in additional leadership courses offered by John C. Maxwell, including *The 15 Invaluable Laws of Growth, The 21 Irrefutable Laws of Leadership, and Developing the Leader Within You.* Through these, I learned that leadership is about setting direction and having the ability to guide, inspire, and mo-tivate people to work collaboratively and effectively.

What I've Engaged In and Learned from These Immersions:

I developed self-awareness skills using tools such as the MBTI, the Emotional Intelligence (EQ) test, and the DISC assessment. These tools helped me identify my leadership style and the characteristics that allow me to better understand my thoughts, emotions, and behaviors in becoming a sustainable leader.

The EQ-i model of emotional intelligence truly pre-pared me for several aspects of leadership. This test fo-cused on my ability and tendency to grow, be self-directed, acknowledge my needs and thoughts, give and receive trust, assess the present moment, and cooperate and contribute to the welfare of a larger social system. This was the first step in building sustainable leadership. I needed to understand myself before I could effectively cultivate growth within my team and organization.

EQ focused on areas such as:

- Self-Perception – self-regard, self-actualization, and emotional self-awareness
- Self-Expression – emotional expression, assertiveness, and independence
- Stress Management – flexibility, stress tolerance, and optimism
- Decision-Making – problem-solving, reality testing, and impulse control
- Interpersonal–Relationships, empathy, and social responsibility

I scored high in self-awareness. However, I needed to develop my decision-making skills. The most helpful skills I learned were: developing stress tolerance, staying composed under pressure, and building confidence by trusting my ability to make sound decisions. Time management also became a key factor in improving my decision-making. I began allocating my time more wisely to support effective choices.

Another assessment that provided insight into my leadership style was the DISC Assessment (Dominant–Driver, Influencing–Inspiring, Stable–Steady, Compliant –Correct). As John C. Maxwell states in *The 15 Invaluable Laws of Growth, "The Law of Awareness: You must know yourself to grow yourself."*

DISC helped me:

- Apply the Law of Awareness to recognize my strengths and limitations
- Overcome shortcomings and clear the path for personal and professional goals
- Understand how others are different and how to work effectively with each personality type
- Build a stronger team that communicates well, appreciates differences, and works collaboratively
- Learn strategies for handling conflict and managing personality clashes
- Develop myself and others to be their best

You may wonder how this is relevant to avoiding burnout and cultivating growth. Here's what I learned about myself, so keep reading.

My DISC style is predominantly "SCI–Advocate," meaning I prefer receiving information in a way that allows me to feel part of a team. However, when communicating that same information to a client or coworker, I may need to translate it into precise facts or focus on just the result. That assessment helped me validate my strengths and identify areas for improvement. I share this valuable information to encourage you to do the same. Find that missing piece to help you avoid burnout and cultivate growth.

A dominant "S" style may not voice their opinions as readily as others around them, yet those same others often value their input deeply.

In the Workplace:

The high-S style is someone you can depend on to use common sense and follow through. S-style employees are responsible, loyal, steady, easygoing, and friendly.

S-styles find ways to balance the demands of both tasks and people. Their practical nature takes care of business without sacrificing relationships. This proficiency makes them excellent managers, directors, supervisors, and administrators of people, projects, and operations.

I've shared several tools that have helped me cultivate growth and find confidence in my leadership role. Confidence as a leader is a powerful and essential quality that inspires trust,

> **"CONFIDENCE...INSPIRES TRUST, DRIVES EFFECTIVE DECISION-MAKING, AND POSITIVELY INFLUENCES OTHERS. "**

drives effective decision-making, and positively influences others. This confidence is grounded in self-awareness, experience, and a willingness to grow. It is the belief in your ability to lead others effectively. It's not arrogance, it's a reflection of grounded awareness and growth.

It became clearer that leadership confidence is essential. The key traits of leadership confidence include:

- Clarity in communication
- Decisiveness under pressure
- Willingness to take responsibility
- Authenticity and integrity
- Emotional resilience

I agree that confidence matters in leadership because it can:

- Inspire trust: People follow leaders who appear confident and self-assured.
- Boost morale: A confident leader uplifts the team, especially during challenges.
- Improve decision-making: Confidence supports quicker, clearer decisions.
- Encourage innovation: Confident leaders are not afraid to try new things.

To sustain a leadership role, I needed to address the areas that had eroded my confidence and my ability to cultivate and maintain growth, as well as develop the skills to overcome these challenges.

1. Imposter Syndrome: Keep a success journal
2. Fear of Criticism: Learn to separate self-worth from feedback
3. Perfectionism: Aim for progress, not perfection
4. Over-comparison: Focus on your growth and mission

I agree that some new leaders possess the skills and know-how to tackle such an important role, while others require significant support. Now that I am in a different leadership capacity, experienced burnout, completed my self-assessments, and identified my personality traits, I can share why leadership can lead to burnout.

Why Leadership Can Lead to Burnout:
- High Responsibility: Leaders are accountable not

only for their work but also for the performance and well-being of their team. That pressure can be relentless.

- Emotional Labor: Supporting, motivating, and managing people, especially during tough times, can be emotionally draining.
- Decision Fatigue: Constantly making essential decisions can wear down mental reserves, especially when decisions involve conflict or uncertainty.
- Isolation: Leadership can be a lonely experience. Leaders may feel they cannot be vulnerable or share their struggles, which can compound stress.
- Work-Life Imbalance: Leaders often work long hours and may struggle to "switch off," especially in fast-paced or high-stakes environments.

In my past role as a chief nurse, I reviewed this concise list of reasons why leadership can contribute to burnout. The primary reasons for my burnout were the high level of responsibility and decision fatigue, which ultimately impacted my work-life balance. The responsibility to ensure that healthcare providers were trained to provide safe care caused sleepless nights.

But It Doesn't Have to Be That Way:
Leaders who set boundaries, delegate effectively, and cultivate emotional intelligence tend to fare better. Here are a few protective factors:

- Self-awareness and recognizing early signs of burnout
- Strong support systems like mentors, peers, and coaches
- An organizational culture that values well-being, not just productivity
- Time management and the ability to say no

Leadership doesn't guarantee burnout, but the risk is real, especially if leaders aren't proactive about protecting their well-being. Throughout various segments of my leadership career, I experienced some of the signs of burnout listed below. Becoming self-aware was the first step to acknowledging them.

Physical Signs:
- Fatigue or low energy, even after rest
- Headaches, muscle tension
- Changes in sleep or appetite

Emotional Signs:
- Feeling overwhelmed or emotionally drained
- Loss of motivation or sense of purpose

Behavioral Signs:
- Withdrawing from team or social interaction
- Procrastinating or avoiding decisions
- Difficulty focusing or making mistakes

What Does Leadership Strategy Entail?
A leadership strategy is a set of methods, tactics, and

attitudes used by leaders to guide and motivate their teams and align them with organizational goals. It allows the organization's culture and value system to align with ideas and impact, creating a mental and emotional influence with far-reaching consequences. An effective leadership strategy provides a structured vision that sets team members and senior management on the path to success and productivity. Now that I've covered burnout and leadership strategies, let's look further into sustained leadership. When I reflect on my leadership role, I ask myself what gives me energy and what drains me.

I ask you:

- Do you exercise regularly?
- Do you have a daily quiet time or practice meditation?
- Do you engage in self-reflection?
- How about talking with a mentor or peer?
- Lastly, do you celebrate small wins?

Sustained leadership is no walk in the park, but it can be transformed into a well-oiled machine. Sustainable Leadership refers to a leadership approach that balances the long-term health of people, the organization, and the environment. It's about making ethical, future-focused, and resilient decisions while fostering well-being, equity, and systemic impact.

Sustained Leadership refers to a consistent and reliable display of leadership qualities over time. It conveys the idea that someone doesn't just act like a leader in isolated moments but demonstrates long-term commitment, vision, and influence that earns the respect and trust of others.

Sustained leadership enhances employee retention and satisfaction, fosters a stronger reputation and brand trust, and drives greater innovation and long-term profitability. It's about walking the talk, aligning words with actions, and maintaining ethical standards, even under pressure.

How many times have we seen leaders fail these vital steps when charged with difficult decisions, especially if it requires the company to right-size? Many changes and uncertainties can cause employees to feel anxious and unstable.

Here are a few key principles of sustainable leadership:

- Long-Term Thinking
  - Focus on legacy, continuity, and future generations.
  - Avoid short-term fixes in favor of lasting impact.

- Ethical and Responsible Decision-Making
  - Operate with integrity, transparency, and social responsibility.
  - Consider the broader implications of business practices.

- People-Centeredness
  - Prioritize employee well-being, growth, and engagement.

○ Encourage diversity, inclusion, and psychological safety.

- Systemic Awareness
  ○ Lead beyond the organization, impacting industry and community.

- Resilience and Adaptability
  ○ Build cultures that thrive through change.
  ○ Encourage learning, innovation, and agility.

Here are some tips on how to practice sustained leadership:
- Integrate sustainability into vision and strategy.
- Invest in leadership development and emotional intelligence.
- Create feedback loops for continuous improvement.
- Collaborate with stakeholders for shared value.

Now that we've discussed self-awareness, burnout, and sustained leadership, let's explore cultivating growth. There is no silver bullet antidote. Employing a multipronged approach that includes strategies to help managers recover from burnout can lead to increased and sustained growth.

Cultivating Growth:
The remedy for cultivating growth is not an instantaneous single solution, nor is it a one-size-fits-all. Using the above strategies and tips in combination, over time,

will not only support and recharge you but also help manage the burned-out leader and prevent burnout in the future, leading to sustained leadership.

The workplace is a community or a society that contributes to the sense of the individual in terms of their identity, affiliation, worth, and meaning. Therefore, creating a positive workplace environment that promotes employee well-being is essential to helping employees handle the stressors involved with both work and life.

Mitigating burnout through participation in recovery experiences fosters a positive work environment where employees experience fulfillment in both their professional and personal lives, ultimately leading to sustained growth.

> "SUSTAINED GROWTH IN LEADERSHIP ENTAILS A LIFELONG COMMITMENT TO LEARNING, EVOLVING, AND POSITIVELY INFLUENCING OTHERS."

Sustained growth in leadership refers to the continuous development and evolution of a person's leadership capabilities over time. It's not just about having leadership skills but also about actively refining, expanding, and applying them consistently to meet new challenges, inspire others, and drive meaningful impact.

Sustained growth in leadership entails a lifelong commitment to learning, evolving, and positively influencing others while remaining grounded in values, driven by purpose, and open to change.

Some Core Aspects of Sustained Growth in Leadership:

- Regularly evaluates strengths, weaknesses, and

leadership style
- Seeks and accepts feedback with openness
- Practices humility and acknowledges areas for growth
- Invests in personal and professional development
- Stays current with leadership trends, tools, and strategies
- Coaches emerging leaders and builds succession plans
- Focuses on lasting impact, not just personal achievement

Resilience in Leadership:

As I conclude this chapter, I find that resilience in leadership is a rich and essential theme that explores how leaders sustain their strength, adapt under pressure, and guide others through uncertainty. It is the ability to recover quickly from setbacks while remaining grounded and effective during times of change.

As leaders, we must cultivate optimism, anchoring ourselves in a hopeful, forward-focused mindset, while fostering a team culture grounded in mutual support, even amid burnout. To do this effectively, we need a clear, holistic understanding of our team's strengths, struggles, and needs. That understanding allows us to guide a team through a challenge.

Final questions:
1. When was the last time you demonstrated resilience?
2. What healthy boundaries have you developed to

lead more effectively?

3. What lessons have you learned from failure?

So, back to the original question: Does leadership and burnout go hand in hand? I encourage you to explore your thoughts and experiences before answering.

CHAPTER 14

LEGACY THROUGH LEVERAGE:

THE MULTIPLIER EFFECT OF MENTORSHIP, SPONSORSHIP & STRATEGIC NETWORKS

Angela Jackson-Andrews

The Leadership Journey: You Were Never Meant to Climb Alone

In the early years of my corporate career, I found myself navigating a landscape filled with unspoken rules, invisible barriers, and relentless pressure to perform. I was determined, driven, and deeply committed to excellence, but I was also doing it alone. I hadn't yet realized that being capable wasn't the same as being visible. There was a difference between adding value and being seen.

I entered the insurance industry without a formal leadership title, but I was leading nonetheless. Through initiative, integrity, and consistent execution, I became someone others relied on, not because of authority, but because of trust and consistency. I learned to solve complex problems under pressure, communicate with clarity, and deliver results that mattered. That season became a powerful training ground and foundation in my career, sharpening not only my skills but also my resolve. It taught me that leadership is not given, it's earned, and more importantly, claimed.

Still, as my competence grew, so did a sense of professional isolation. I was producing, contributing, and consistently adding value, but I hadn't yet activated the key multipliers of advancement: mentorship, sponsorship, and strategic networks. I was self-directed in my performance but not in navigating the support pillars of my career. I began to understand that owning your path means being intentional, not just about what you do, but with whom you align. Access isn't given; it's cultivated. No matter how strong your performance, advancement often depends on who's advocating for you when you're not in the room.

Looking back, I understand a truth I didn't yet have the language for: Success isn't just about capability, it's about connection. It's not only about performance but also positioning. It's never solely about effort; it's about elevation, and the people who help lift you there. Talent may unlock the door, but visibility earns you an invitation, and advocacy ensures you cross the threshold.

The missing pieces were mentors who saw me, sponsors who spoke on my behalf, and strategic networks that supported my climb. I had mastered performance, but I hadn't activated the relationships that multiply influence and expand access. I was capable, but I wasn't connected.

Brilliance matters, but it's amplified through alignment. You can exceed every expectation, but if no one speaks your name in the rooms where decisions are made, your brilliance may remain hidden in plain sight. I've learned that being self-directed isn't just about how you show up; it's about who you align with, how intentionally you cultivate visibility, and the clarity with which you design your leadership journey. There is power in partnership, transformation in being seen, and legacy in lifting others as you rise.

The Truth Behind the Closed Door: Stories, Not Spreadsheets

Once I understood what was missing, I began to view my leadership path through a different lens, one sharpened by self-direction and a deeper awareness of what advancement truly requires. A few years later, still early in my career, I was promoted to the Talent Development Team as a corporate management trainer—a formal leadership role aligned with my passion for growth, people, and purpose. That role was

> "THERE IS POWER IN PARTNERSHIP, TRANSFORMATION IN BEING SEEN, AND LEGACY IN LIFTING OTHERS AS YOU RISE."

more than a promotion; it was a transformation. I wasn't just facilitating learning, I was equipping future leaders to show up with impact, confidence, and clarity at the highest levels.

Then came the meeting that would forever shift my perspective. I was invited to attend my first talent development strategy session. The room was filled with VPs, senior executives, and HR decision-makers. I came prepared for a conversation centered on metrics: dashboards, development plans, and performance trends. What unfolded was far more revealing.

The discussions weren't about spreadsheets; they were about stories. Executives spoke names and shared narratives that elevated visibility, affirmed readiness, and opened doors to new opportunities. It was at that moment that I understood the truth behind the closed door: careers weren't just being evaluated, they were being designed.

That's when it clicked. People weren't advancing solely because they performed well. They were being elevated because they were remembered, spoken for, and associated with potential. Someone with power and proximity chose to say their name, share their story, champion their advancement, and stake their reputation on their rise.

> **"TALENT WITHOUT TRACTION STALLS, AND BRILLIANCE WITHOUT ADVOCACY REMAINS INVISIBLE."**

This experience shaped my mission. Today, I help organizations and leaders build the kinds of relationships that multiply impact: mentors who challenge and refine, sponsors who advocate and position, and networks that sustain and support. Talent without traction stalls, and brilliance without advocacy remains invisible. Leaders don't just rise because they are ready; they rise when someone opens the door and says, "They're next."

If you're waiting for your work to speak for itself, consider this: voices move faster than metrics. No matter how talented or prepared you are, your advancement often depends on who is willing to tell your story when you're not in the room. Performance is your foundation, but relationships are the runway.

The question isn't just, "Are you ready?" It's, "Who knows you're ready, and who's willing to say it out loud?"

The Paradigm Shift: The Myth of the Solo Climb

For too long, leadership was defined by individualism: keep your head down, grind harder, and let your results speak. We were told to prove ourselves in isolation, trusting that someone would eventually take notice, but that mindset is more than outdated; it's a leadership liability. It reflects a systemic blind spot that undervalues the power of advocacy, connection, and intentional support.

The truth is, leadership is not a solo sport. Isolation breeds burnout, stagnation, and underutilized potential. Burnout doesn't always stem from doing too much; it often comes from carrying the weight alone, without a mentor to guide you, a sponsor to position you, or an ally to stand with you.

"LEADERSHIP IS NOT A SOLO SPORT."

Today's most effective leaders elevate differently. They deliver results, but they also understand that strategic alliances are not optional; they're essential. Relationship-building isn't a soft skill; it's a core leadership competency. Waiting for a tap on the shoulder delays your trajectory. Connection, visibility, and advocacy aren't just desirable; they are the pillars of leadership positioning and power.

The Data Speaks

We've all heard the phrase, "Let the data speak for itself." The data doesn't just speak, it shouts a reality many professionals live but rarely voice: the playing field isn't level, and talent alone doesn't always rise. If you've ever felt unseen despite your results, you're not imagining it. The numbers back it up. *McKinsey & Company's 2023 Report* found that for every 100 men promoted to manager, only 87 women—and just 73 women of color—make that same leap. The gap doesn't begin in the boardroom; it begins at the very first rung of leadership. This isn't about ability, it's about access.

Harvard Business Review reinforces this truth: professionals with sponsors are 23% more likely to be promoted. Yet, only 23% of professionals report having a sponsor at all. That means the very thing that could change the trajectory of someone's career is one of the most underutilized tools in the workplace. Sponsorship isn't a luxury; it's a leadership imperative.

"DATA TELLS A STORY, BUT YOUR LEADERSHIP JOURNEY IS YOURS TO AUTHOR."

LinkedIn's 2023 insights add another layer: 85% of jobs are filled through networking, not applications or algorithms, but through relationships. Access is often granted through connection, and strategic relationships remain one of the most powerful leadership resources.

If we are serious about cultivating diverse, dynamic leadership, we must reimagine the systems that define advancement. That means making mentorship purposeful, normalizing sponsorship as a core leadership practice, and building strategic networks rooted in equity, intention, and action. This is how we shift from potential to positioning, from being capable to being championed. The data tells a story, but your leadership journey is yours to author. The question is: Who's helping you turn the page?

The Invisible Lift: Roles That Raise Leaders

We often assume mentorship and sponsorship are tools reserved only for early-career professionals: foundational support to help find footing and direction. The truth is this: the higher you rise, the more intentional your support system must become.

At the highest levels of leadership, mentorship isn't optional; it's essential. The more accomplished you become, the more critical it is to have people who sharpen your perspective, challenge your blind spots, and believe in your vision even when doubt creeps in. Yet, it often becomes harder to ask for that support the higher you rise. I've seen it across every level I've mentored. High-achieving leaders never outgrow the need for insight, accountability, or advocacy because the pressure, scrutiny, and complexity of problems increase. Elevation is not a one-time event; it's a continuous force fueled by three powerful roles: mentors who refine your mindset, sponsors who expand your access, and networks that stretch your capacity.

> "MENTORS ARE NOT ANSWER–GIVERS, THEY'RE PERSPECTIVE SHAPERS."

Mentors: Wisdom Sharers

Mentors are not answer-givers, they're perspective shapers. They illuminate blind spots, challenge your assumptions, and walk alongside your growth. Great mentors reflect the leader you're becoming even before you fully see it.

They help you reframe failure, reconnect with your core identity, and rediscover confidence when doubt creeps in. They don't just see your résumé, they see your rhythm, your rise, and your resilience.

Sponsors: Strategic Amplifiers

Mentors shape your thinking, but sponsors shape your trajectory. Sponsors don't just believe in your potential; they act on it. They use their voice, platform, and influence to open doors that would otherwise remain closed.

Sponsorship isn't random; it's earned through visibility, credibility, and value. It's built on trust and impact.

Strategic Networks: The Collective Circle

Strategic networks are not just social; they are intentional ecosystems of insight, accountability, and possibility. They include peers, coaches, thought partners, and truth-tellers. These networks multiply your reach, resilience, and relevance.

When built with purpose, your network becomes a circle of capacity, not just connection. Iron sharpens iron, and high-level leaders surround themselves with others who stretch, challenge, and elevate. Together, mentors, sponsors, and networks form your **Lift Circle**, an infrastructure of advocacy, wisdom, and strategic elevation.

Here's the truth, too many leaders overlook: not all mentorship is meaningful, not all sponsorship is strategic, and not all networks are nourishing. As you rise, it becomes even more important to curate your circle with intentionality and clarity. The people around you will either support your climb or quietly cap your potential.

Who surrounds you matters just as much as what drives you.

Take a moment to consider: Who sharpens your thinking? Who speaks your name when you're not in the room? Who stretches your vision, challenges your comfort zone, and reminds you what you're capable of?

As I reflect on my journey, these questions became more than strategic. The moments I experienced my greatest lift were never mine alone. Let me share how I discovered the power of being seen, supported, and stretched.

Where Belief Meets Opportunity: My Story of the Lift

When I stepped into the role of Executive Officer for Talent Development, I earned it through years of consistent performance and purposeful leadership. On paper, I was ready, but internally, impostor syndrome whispered another story: "Can you hold this seat?"

That's when the lift appeared, in real time. My mentor, who had walked with me through many seasons of growth, looked me in the eye and said, "You don't have to prove you belong. Just show up as the leader you already are."

That sentence silenced the noise. It reminded me that readiness isn't about perfection; it's about showing up, believing, and betting on yourself.

Almost simultaneously, the phone rang; it was my sister, the one who has always seen me. From helping me reclaim my literal voice as a child to encouraging me to use that voice to empower others, she has been my mirror, anchor, and constant. Her belief in me never wavered, even when mine did. Her love reminded me, "You weren't just born for this, you've been becoming this all along." At that moment, I realized: The lift isn't only professional. It's personal. It shows up in mentorship, in kinship, and in community.

Becoming the Lift

With elevation comes responsibility. As the Bible states, "To whom much is given, much is required" (Luke 12:48, KJV). The same applies to leadership.

During a talent succession meeting, a rising leader's name surfaced. Her results were strong, but her visibility was low outside of working within her team. The room hesitated. I listened, but no one spoke up. So I did.

"She's a quiet storm. She doesn't just meet goals, she elevates those around her. That's not just performance. That's leadership."

The energy shifted. Her name moved forward. A month later, she was nominated and received a countrywide innovation award for a project she spearheaded. That is what it means to become the lift. It's advocacy in action and leadership in motion.

Mentorship isn't just about offering guidance; it's about illuminating what someone can't yet see in themselves. Sponsorship isn't just about promotion; it's about positioning people to step fully into their power, and networks increase collective capacity, where iron sharpens iron.

Becoming the lift means you no longer wait for the elevator doors of opportunity to open; you design the entire mechanism that elevates yourself and others. It's a mindset shift: from climbing alone to constructing a system of ascent. However, that leads to a critical question: How do we embody this kind of leadership in a world shaped by silos, biases, and invisible barriers?

> "BECOMING THE LIFT MEANS YOU...DESIGN THE ENTIRE MECHANISM THAT ELEVATES YOURSELF AND OTHERS."

That's where the ACCESS comes in. Success doesn't just come from working harder; it comes from having access to opportunity, influence, invisibility, and your voice.

The ACCESS Code™: The Leverage & Leadership Multiplier

The ACCESS Code™ is a strategic guide and framework for becoming the architect of your rise, while unlocking pathways for others. Each letter represents a transformational principle:

A – Advocacy

You don't just need a voice—you need voices in the room when you're not there. Advocacy transforms isolation into elevation. Leadership success requires allies who champion you, name you in critical conversations, and affirm your value when you're not present.

C – Credibility

Your performance opens the door. Your reputation keeps it open. Credibility is earned. It's not just what you say, it's how you show up with consistency, character, and competence.

C – Connection

Leadership is not a solo sport. It's a strategic alliance. Be intentional in building relationships that are both authentic and aligned. Relationships create elevation. Connection isn't just personal, it's a leadership accelerant.

E – Exposure

Visibility is not vanity, it's value. Position yourself where decisions are made. Strategic presence increases trust, familiarity, and the likelihood of opportunity. Let the right people see your value, not just your work. Bring energy, clarity, and confidence in every room you enter.

S – Sponsorship

Mentors give insight. Sponsors give you access. A sponsor doesn't just believe in you; they act on your behalf.

S – Systems of Support

Sustainable leadership requires strong foundations. No one should burn out to succeed. Build systems: people, processes, and practices that support your brilliance.

ACCESS™ is more than a framework; it's a call to disrupt invisibility, rewrite outdated rules, and take radical ownership of your rise. It's about setting the standard for what transformational leadership looks like. You don't need permission. ACCESS™ has already been granted.

The Rise Begins Within

Having mentors, sponsors, and aligned strategic networks is a powerful leadership accelerator, but only when leveraged with intention and integrity. Still, the truth is:

No mentor can do the work for you. No sponsor can shape a vision you haven't claimed. No network can open a door you're not prepared to walk through.

Access doesn't replace responsibility; it multiplies your impact when you bring self-awareness, clarity, and purpose to the table.

Leadership begins with you:

Owning your growth

Stewarding your voice.

Rising in a way that makes room for others.

> **"POWER SHARED IS POWER MULTIPLIED."**

To activate **ACCESS**™ to its highest potential, embody these six anchors:

- Awareness of your unique value and the barriers that may exist
- Clarity on what you want and why it matters
- Connection that is both authentic and strategic
- Elevation that lifts others as you rise
- Strategy that aligns your actions with your aspirations
- Sustainability that ensures your rise doesn't cost you your wellness or your legacy

The future belongs to leaders who understand: Power shared is power multiplied. Mentorship lights the path. Sponsorship clears the way. Strategic networks remind us that we're never walking alone. You have the model. You have the mirror. Now, bring the movement.

Your Voice. Your Power. Your Rise.

CHAPTER 15

LEADERSHIP LEGACY:
HOW WILL YOU BE REMEMBERED?

Dr. ShaNita Nolan

*T*he first leaders I knew weren't behind podiums or seated at boardroom tables. They were my parents, who taught me the earliest lessons about responsibility and perseverance. However, if leadership could ever be personified in its purest, most enduring form, it was in the quiet strength of my grandmother, Mudeah.

She wasn't a CEO, a director, or an elected official. She didn't carry a title that demanded attention. Yet, when she walked into a room, the very atmosphere shifted. A reverence surrounded her, not one imposed, but one earned. Her leadership didn't require announcements or accolades. It was rooted in unshakable faith, refined by suffering, and defined by a commitment to do what was right, even when it cost her everything.

Mudeah didn't just talk about values; she lived them. She had a way of correcting you without crushing your spirit and guiding you without making you feel small. Her wisdom didn't come from textbooks but from life, raising children through adversity, serving her community without recognition, and holding fast to her faith when others might have faltered.

From her, I learned that leadership is not about commanding others but about commanding your character. It's about being a thermostat, not a thermometer, setting the tone rather than merely reacting to it. Real leaders don't manipulate moments; they mold hearts, and they do it with a steady, humble hand.

Mudeah taught me that real leaders are servants first. They see people not as tools to be used, but as lives to be nurtured. They hold others to high expectations while walking beside them through every struggle. They correct with kindness and celebrate with humility. Watching her, I learned that the foundation of any leadership legacy must be integrity and compassion, welded together by courage.

> "LEADERSHIP IS NOT ABOUT COMMANDING OTHERS BUT ABOUT COMMANDING YOUR CHARACTER."

Under her influence, I first understood the power of living and leading your message. Her life, not just her words, was a blueprint for the kind of leader I aspired to become.

Looking back, I see that Mudeah was building a legacy, one decision, one conversation, one sacrifice at a time. Though her name never appeared in headlines, her impact continues to echo in the lives of those she touched. I am one of them.

Leadership Beyond Titles

Years later, those seeds of servant leadership bloomed as I stepped into my role as a human resources (HR) director. In that capacity, I held a critical role that straddled the organization and its people's interests. I was responsible for managing people and stewarding an organization's conscience. HR leadership, at its core, is not about compliance checklists or benefits packages; it's about people, ethics, and the invisible threads that hold an organization together.

I built a career with integrity, character, and excellence. I took pride in being the person executives and employees could count on. I wasn't the loudest voice in the room, but I was consistent and intentional. I believed every policy should serve a purpose, and every employee deserved to be seen.

Under my leadership, the HR department and the corporation thrived. I led initiatives that improved workplace morale, streamlined onboarding processes, and elevated professional and leadership development. I was being mentored for promotion to Vice President of Human Resources, a testament to the hard work, vision, and leadership I had poured into the organization.

My leadership excellence and embodiment of the company's core values of Responsibility, Creativity, Integrity, and Collaboration did not go unnoticed. I received a sizable monetary award and was publicly recognized at a corporate awards ceremony. This acknowledgment reaffirmed my belief that leading with integrity and compassion leaves an indelible mark.

One day, while conducting what I assumed would be a routine compliance audit, I stumbled upon data that stopped me cold. There were patterns, deeply troubling ones, that revealed discriminatory practices, pay inequities, and unethical behaviors that violated not only company policy but also federal law.

I wish I could say I was shocked, but I wasn't. I had seen hints of it before, whispers in the break room, glances exchanged during meetings, but this time, I had irrefutable evidence.

A Defining Crossroads

I sat with that evidence for a moment that felt like forever. There is a silence that descends when you're standing at a moral crossroads, a stillness where every value you've ever claimed is put on trial. In that moment, I heard Mudeah's voice, not audibly, but internally, rising like a lighthouse in a storm. She had always said, "Integrity is doing what's right when no one is clapping."

So, I did what she taught me. I chose to act. I presented the findings to the organization's leadership. I didn't point fingers; I presented solutions. I built an action plan to address the discrepancies, provide training, and protect the company from lawsuits. I believed, naively, perhaps, that truth and transparency would prevail. They didn't.

> "INTEGRITY IS DOING WHAT'S RIGHT WHEN NO ONE IS CLAPPING."

My efforts were met with indifference, resistance, and hostility. Although I faced undeniable pressure to conform, I consciously decided to remain aligned with my values. I chose to stand, quietly but firmly, for what was right. I chose integrity.

The Price of Integrity

What followed was a campaign to strip me of authority, tarnish my reputation, and pressure me into submission. My professional standing was systematically dismantled, but I remained resolute.

Leadership, authentic leadership, doesn't exist only when hope is easy. When faced with the deterioration of my role and the challenges to my integrity, I leaned harder than ever on the principles Mudeah had embodied: grace, humility, resilience, and unwavering ethical courage.

I refused to retaliate. I refused to compromise. I refused to allow bitterness to define me. What I didn't realize at the time was that my team was watching.

> **"LEADERSHIP...DOESN'T EXIST ONLY WHEN HOPE IS EASY."**

They saw the attacks, but more importantly, they saw my response. I didn't retaliate. I didn't gossip. I didn't let bitterness take root. I showed up every day with my head high, doing excellent work, refusing to let adversity rewrite my narrative.

One afternoon, a young staff member slipped into my office, closed the door behind her, and with tears in her eyes said, "I've never seen anyone lead like this before. You've made me believe it's possible to lead and still be good."

That moment was worth every wound.

The Ripple Effect of Leadership

Leadership is never a solo act. It creates ripples that outlive our tenure, outlast our titles, and outshine any temporary recognition. After I eventually left the organization, I wrestled with doubt. Had it been worth it? Had I made a difference? In time, the answer came, not through awards or headlines, but through the people.

Former colleagues reached out. They told me how

my decision to stand in integrity helped them find their voice. Some left their toxic roles. Others launched initiatives to advocate for fairness in their teams. Many simply said, "You reminded me of who I want to be."

Leadership is not about being remembered by the masses. It's about being remembered by "the one"– the one person who watched, who learned, who changed because you chose to lead with courage.

The Anatomy of Resilience

My journey didn't end in that chapter; it simply turned a page. I had to rebuild. Not just my career, but my confidence, my identity, and my sense of purpose. The dismantling of my professional role had the potential to break me, but it didn't, because what they couldn't strip away was my calling.

> "LEADERSHIP IS... ABOUT BEING REMEMBERED BY THE 'ONE'."

Resilience is not a one-time event. It is the daily decision to rise, over and over, while still choosing grace. I returned to my roots. I poured my pain into purpose. I began speaking, mentoring, and writing, helping other leaders navigate their storms with integrity and faith.

Every setback became a seed. Every disappointment became soil for something greater to grow. I was no longer just building a career; I was building a legacy.

Integrity Under Fire

There's a difference between reputation and character. Reputation is what people think you are; character is what God knows you to be. Operating with integrity under fire means choosing character over comfort. Even in environments where toxicity thrives, where deceit is rewarded, and where truth is inconvenient, I chose excellence.

I continued to give my best not because I was being watched, but because I was accountable to Someone higher. Leadership, when done right, costs something, but it also yields something far greater than recognition: it yields peace.

The Legacy You Leave

When all is said and done, when the nameplate is removed, the inbox is empty, and the seat at the table is filled by someone else, what will remain?

Your leadership legacy won't be found in your title or your LinkedIn profile. It will be found in the lives you touched, the courage you showed, and the truth you stood for when it mattered most.

Titles, salaries, or accolades do not determine leadership; it is measured by who you lifted, what values you upheld, and how deeply you impacted those who walked beside you.

So, when your leadership story is told, how will you be remembered? Your legacy is being written right now with every conversation, decision, apology, and act of courage. Write yours well.

A Daily Compass for Legacy-Minded Leaders

As leadership expert John C. Maxwell shares in his book Intentional Living: Choosing a Life That Matters, legacy is not a single moment; it's crafted daily through intentional reflection and action. He encourages leaders to pause regularly and ask:

- What did I do today that added value to someone?
- What will I be remembered for if today were my last?
- Who am I mentoring or developing right now?

These questions aren't just reflective, they're directional. They recalibrate your heart and leadership to align with the legacy you desire to leave.

The Influence You Never See

Years after leaving that organization, I was invited to speak at a leadership summit for emerging professionals. It was one of those full-circle moments, standing in front of ambitious, driven individuals who were just beginning their journey and reminding them that leadership isn't a destination but a daily decision.

"FEAR IS REAL, BUT SO IS YOUR LEGACY." After my keynote, a young woman approached me with a notebook full of notes and eyes full of questions. She said, "You talked about leading with integrity even when it costs you something, but what if you're just starting and you're afraid of being blacklisted, misunderstood, or dismissed?"

I looked at her and saw a version of myself, years earlier, staring down a decision that would define me. I told her, "Fear is real, but so is your legacy. One day, you will look back and realize that your most courageous moments were the ones that shaped your influence. The only question is, will you choose comfort, or will you choose impact?"

Her shoulders lifted slightly, and I watched a seed of courage take root. That's the thing about leadership. Often, you don't see the impact immediately. You don't get applause for doing the right thing, but the ripple continues.

As Warren Bennis said, "Leadership is the capacity to translate vision into reality." But that vision must first be internal, built on values you refuse to abandon.

Mentoring Through the Fire

One of the most humbling chapters in my career came during a mentorship program I was asked to co-lead for a cohort of first-generation college graduates entering the workforce. Many of them came from under-resourced communities. Their résumés were solid, but their confidence was shaky.

> "TRUE BELONGING ISN'T FOUND IN PERFECTION, IT'S FOUND IN THE COURAGE TO BE AUTHENTIC."

One young man in particular, David, stood out. He was brilliant, analytical, quiet, and paralyzed by impostor syndrome. During our second session, he opened up: "I'm afraid I'll mess up, that I don't belong here, that they'll find out I'm not good enough."

I sat with his vulnerability, and I shared mine. I recounted the moment I stood alone in the boardroom, my voice trembling as I spoke my truth. I described the nights spent sobbing in my car, grappling with the loss of community and comfort that came from choosing integrity over convenience. I shared the heartbreak of enduring a miscarriage, brought on by the overwhelming stress of my job. I revealed the hard-won lesson that changed everything: True belonging isn't found in perfection, it's found in the courage to be authentic.

Over the months, I watched David transform. He began speaking up more, asking better questions, and volunteering for leadership opportunities. At the end of the program, he said, "You helped me see that courage isn't the absence of fear, it's showing up anyway."

That's what legacy looks like in real time. Not applause, but awakening. Not followers, but leaders in the making.

The Character You Carry

There's an old saying: "Your talent can take you places your character can't keep you."

> "CHARACTER IS HOW YOU MAKE PEOPLE FEEL WHEN NO ONE'S LOOKING."

How true that is. We've all seen it: leaders who rise fast but fall hard because their foundation was built on sand. Flashy résumés, impressive titles, but behind closed doors, they cut corners, manipulate outcomes, or treat people like transactions. Their legacy? Shattered trust. I never wanted that.

I would rather move slower and sleep in peace than race ahead by compromising my values. Leadership is not about climbing; it's about carrying: carrying people, carrying purpose, carrying responsibility, even when it's heavy.

As Maya Angelou once said, "People will forget what you said, people will forget what you did, but people will never forget how you made them feel."

Character is how you make people feel when no one's looking. It's the tone of your emails, the humility in your corrections, and the consistency in your convictions.

Choosing Resilience Over Reputation

I've had moments when I wanted to walk away from leadership altogether; times when I questioned whether it was worth it to keep choosing the high road while others profited from shortcuts. Every time, I came back to one truth: My integrity is not situational, it's foundational. Resilience isn't just bouncing back; it's choosing not to become the very thing that broke you.

While rebuilding my career, I also had to rebuild my identity. For years, my role was my reputation, and my title was my introduction. When that was taken, I was left with the core of who I was, and I realized that was enough.

I had wisdom, experience, and vision. Most of all, I had a story that could serve others. So, I began to speak, coach, and mentor, not from a place of perfection, but from a place of refinement. My leadership was no longer about climbing; it was about cultivating. It was also no longer about impressing; it was about impacting.

Building Legacy in the Marketplace

Today's workplace is evolving, with remote work, AI advancements, and generational shifts. However, the need for principled leadership has never been greater. Employees are looking not just for bosses but for emotionally intelligent, morally grounded, and courageously authentic leaders. They're watching how you handle failure, how well you listen, and how you navigate ambiguity and adversity. They want to know: Can I trust you? Do you see me? Will you fight for what's right, even when it's hard?

Legacy in the marketplace isn't built through motivational posters and performance reviews. It's built through everyday interactions: honoring commitments, addressing microaggressions, promoting equity, and modeling self-awareness.

In one organization I consulted, we started a "Leadership Legacy" initiative. It was not a program, but an attempt to shift culture. We asked every leader to define their leadership legacy in one sentence. At first, they struggled, but over time, the statements came:

- "I want to be remembered as someone who made people feel safe enough to grow."
- "I want to lead in a way that outlives my presence."
- "I want my leadership to create more leaders, not more followers."

That's when I knew they had gotten it.

A Final Reflection

As I reflect on my journey, from watching Mudeah serve with quiet grace to standing in boardrooms with truth on my tongue, I see leadership as sacred. It is not a right; it is a responsibility. Leaders don't just carry vision, they impact lives, wield influence, and see possibility. In a world that desperately needs light, our leadership can cast shadows or shine truth.

So, let me ask you again: When your leadership story is told, how will you be remembered? Will your legacy be one of compromise or conviction, convenience or character? You're writing it now.

> **"LEADERS DON'T JUST CARRY VISION, THEY IMPACT LIVES, WIELD INFLUENCE, AND SEE POSSIBILITY."**

With every boundary you set, every apology you offer, every time you choose integrity over image, you are leaving your mark. As John C. Maxwell wisely said, "Leadership is not about titles, positions, or flowcharts. It is about one life influencing another."

May your life, your leadership legacy, be the kind that influences for good. Write your legacy well.

Legacy in Real Life

Not long ago, I was coaching a senior leader on the verge of burnout. She had spent years climbing the ladder, promotion after promotion, recognition after recognition. Yet, in our first session, she looked at me tiredly and said, "I've built a career, but I'm not sure I've built a legacy."

That statement stayed with me. We began unpacking what legacy meant to her. She realized that while she had accomplished a lot, she had rarely paused to consider the wake she was leaving behind. Was she empowering others? Did people feel seen in her presence? Would anyone remember her for how she made them feel? Those questions shifted everything.

Together, we worked not on strategy decks or performance metrics, but on influence, self-awareness, courage, and authenticity. She began mentoring new managers, initiating listening circles with her staff, and ending every team meeting with the question, "What did we learn together today?"

A year later, she told me, "This is the most fulfilling chapter of my career, and it's not about me anymore."

That's the power of reflection. That's the power of legacy-minded leadership.

A Personal Charge to You

I want to leave you with this: You don't have to be perfect to leave a legacy, you just have to be intentional. You don't need a title to make a difference. You don't need a platform to be influential. What you need is clarity, consistency, and courage:

- Clarity about who you are and what you stand for.
- Consistency in how you treat people, show up, and lead.
- Courage to do the right thing, especially when it's the hardest thing.

Take a Moment to Reflect:

- What values are you living out loud?
- Who is better because you crossed paths?
- If today were the last day of your career, what would people say about you?

Let your answers to those questions guide your next

steps. Your leadership matters. Your legacy matters. Your leadership matters whether you lead in an office, on a team, in a classroom, from a pulpit, or at a kitchen table. Your voice, your influence, and your example matter.

When your chapter is finished, when your season comes to a close, may it be said of you:

They led with courage.

They stood for truth.

They built others up.

They didn't just hold a position; they fulfilled a purpose.

That is a leadership legacy. That is how you'll be remembered, and that, my friend, is worth every step of the journey.

Closing Reflections

*L*eadership is not merely a role; it is a relationship between people, with purpose, and through presence. Throughout this anthology, we've pulled back the curtain on leadership as it's lived - not polished, not perfect, but powerful in its vulnerability and clarity. Each contributor has shared not just knowledge, but wisdom earned through experience, evolution, and engagement.

From accountability to inclusion, from mindset to mission, these pages have spotlighted the kind of leadership the world needs now; human, humbler, and wholly committed to impact. If you walk away with one truth, let it be this: Leadership is something you grow into; it's something you choose to grow daily.

We hope this collection challenged your thinking, validated your experiences, and fueled your growth. Carry it forward. Share what you've learned, and most of all, lead in a way that unveils the best in others. When leadership is unveiled, so is potential.

Keep the Momentum Going

If this book moved you, challenged you, or inspired a shift in how you lead, don't keep it to yourself. Share it with your network, your team, and your fellow leaders. Let's spread the movement. To stay connected with the authors and explore upcoming opportunities, from live trainings and keynotes to leadership masterminds, certification courses, and book signings, visit:

www.LeadershipUnveiled.events

There's more ahead. This book is just the beginning.

Meet
the
Authors

ANGELA HOOPER-MENIFIELD, MPA, SPHR, SCP
THE VISIONARY

 Angela Hooper-Menifield, MPA, SPHR, SHRM-SCP, is an Amazon best-selling author, leadership strategist, certified executive coach, and founder of Menifield & Associates, LLC, a consulting and training firm equipping leaders and organizations to thrive when every move matters. With over 28 years of federal leadership experience, including leading a team of 4,000 employees across 14 states, Angela has earned a national reputation for her ability to transform chaos into clarity and potential into performance.

She is the visionary and lead author of *Leadership Unveiled: Elevating Leadership Through Experience,* where she curates and contributes to stories that spotlight leadership in action. Angela is also the founder of *Design, Not Default Publishing™,* a platform built to amplify purpose-driven voices who are ready to share their message with boldness and intention. Whether through books, keynotes, or training, her mission is to empower leaders to stop living by default and instead design lives—and legacies—they're proud of.

Angela is the creator of the *MOVE™ Framework* and *Get Your ACT Together™* methodology, guiding individuals through mindset shifts and meaningful action. She believes leadership isn't a title, it's a decision to lead with Awareness, Clarity, and Tools. Her passion lies in helping others unlock their next chapter with confidence, compassion, and purpose.

DR. CHERYL BURTON

Have you ever had that exhilarating moment when inspiration strikes or a new level of awareness illuminates your thoughts, or when you feel yourself gradually opening to possibilities you once resisted or never imagined? These are the moments experienced by Dr. Cheryl Burton's clients over the past 40 years. These moments continue to inspire and motivate her. They fuel her unyielding passion for encouraging, equipping, and empowering individuals to lead, learn, and live lives of purpose and significance.

As a psychotherapist, coach, and neuroencoding specialist, Dr. Cheryl guides individuals through transformative journeys, helping them uncover insights that spark personal growth and self-empowerment. Her work is grounded in the belief that each of us is created fully resourced and equipped to design the life we desire and become who we were meant to be.

Deeply passionate about helping women navigate difficult life transitions, Dr. Cheryl, a licensed clinical social worker, founded *LeadHerShip™ International*, a revolutionary program designed to help women rediscover their authentic selves, give voice to their desires and dreams, and design a new, self-affirming chapter in life. She believes in the resilience of the human spirit and works to help her clients eliminate self-defeating beliefs and behaviors, access their inner resources, and express themselves in healthy, empowered ways.

Dr. Cheryl is one of the most empowering, charismatic, and captivating voices in motivational speaking today. An international keynote speaker, workshop facilitator, and visionary leader, she has championed personal empowerment and resilience throughout her distinguished career. She has been recognized by numerous professional, civic, and religious organizations for her leadership, commitment, and contributions to her community.

She is also an Executive Director with The Maxwell Leadership Certified Team and a certified DISC Behavioral Analysis Consultant.

In her chapter, "The Leader Within", Dr. Cheryl's goal is to help readers understand that leadership is learned, and that self-leadership is the key to becoming an effective leader. One cannot truly lead others without first learning to lead oneself.

LESLIE BRITT

 My name is Leslie Britt, and I am the CEO of Leslie Britt Enterprise, LLC. I coach from the pillars of vision, mindset, and strategy. After 24 years in the United States Navy, I transitioned to civilian life as a contractor and federal employee. However, I soon realized that the mission-driven environment and camaraderie of military life were missing in the civilian workforce. Many of my friends shared similar feelings of unfulfillment as they sought meaningful roles after service.

Through coaching, I discovered my vision and purpose: to serve others at the highest level, helping them achieve clarity in their vision, mindset, and strategy for life. My goal is to ignite the vision within everyone, turning it into a compelling purpose and a legacy worth living. For those I coach, achieving that "aha moment" and experiencing true transformation unlocks their potential in countless areas of life. I encourage you to step beyond the daily norm and nurture your dreams, ensuring they don't wither away. Finding purpose in civilian life often requires time and support.

This project allows me to share the values of a loving father that have served me in various situations as I've traveled the world and worked with many different people of various ideologies and cultures. It also allows me to pass on what I've learned—and currently live—to my son, so he can share it with his friends, the family he'll have one day, and with those he meets along the journey of life.

DR. ROBIN K. BUTLER

Dr. Robin K. Butler stands as a beacon of transformation in both personal and professional development. Her unwavering commitment to the "Transform ≠ Conform" mantra reflects her fervor for igniting positive change within individuals, students, and organizations, steering them toward thriving and prosperous futures.

With over 25 years of progressive experience in human resources, organizational, and leadership development, Robin leverages her strategic insights to help individuals and organizations enrich communication, reduce conflict, encourage connection, and enhance collaboration. Her toolkit includes the Catalyst 4C (Foresee) Model—an integrated framework comprising Coaching, Conversations, Courses, and Consulting—customized to empower both individuals and organizations.

Building on her experience in leadership development, training and education, employee relations, engagement, and retention, Robin has found her niche as a culture concierge. She partners with corporations, classrooms, and congregations to cultivate and champion culture, integrating her skills as a Certified Human Behavior Consultant and Emotional Intelligence Facilitator. Her impact also reaches academia, where she imparts wisdom as an adjunct professor, shaping the minds of future leaders.

Her guiding philosophy, encapsulated in the acronym H.E.A.R.T. (Honesty, Equity, Accountability, Resiliency, and Transparency), resonates in every endeavor. Dr. Robin epitomizes leadership through development, illuminating pathways to success as she remains committed to leading with intention, influence, and impact.

KENRIC S. LYNN

 Kenric S. Lynn is a certified personal trainer and wellness coach through the National Academy of Sports Medicine, specializing in helping clients get stronger, move better, and live healthier lives. A proud U.S. Army veteran, Kenric served 23 honorable years as a Satellite Communications Systems Operator/Maintainer. He holds an MBA with a concentration in Entrepreneurship from Trident University.

Kenric is a passionate community leader and advocate for veterans. He currently serves as the St. Louis Platoon Leader with The Mission Continues, empowering veterans to serve their communities, and as a volunteer captain with Operation Homefront, which supports military families across the nation.

Believing in the power of entrepreneurship, Kenric champions financial freedom through small business ownership and multiple income streams. He is a licensed Illinois realtor with Century 21 Bailey and Company and Managing Partner of MLP (Mahogany Legacy Project) Capital Advisors, LLC, a financial consultancy supporting small business growth with practical, innovative solutions.

Beyond his professional endeavors, Kenric is a dedicated husband, father, and friend. He enjoys reading, listening to podcasts, and spending quality time with his family. His versatile approach to life reflects his belief in the importance of adaptability and resilience. Kenric lives by the personal motto: "Loving Life, Inspired to Serve, Growing Every Day." Whether leading in the gym, the classroom, or the community, he is committed to empowering others to become the strongest, most resilient versions of themselves.

DR. KATHERINE Y. BAINES BROWN

 Dr. Katherine Y. Brown strives to uplift and inspire others, fostering a belief in their amazingness. She is the author of the bestselling book, *I Am Amazing*. She believes that I Am Amazing will serve as a catalyst for readers to uncover their strength, resilience, and remarkable qualities. Katherine hopes readers will discover that being amazing doesn't rely on external factors or the beliefs of others. These are principles she has instilled in her children and in the hundreds of people she has mentored over the years.

Katherine is a proud mother of four children: Anthony D. Rodgers, Sydney Y. K. Brown, Irving D. Brown, and Robert D. Brown. Born and raised on the South Side of Chicago, her life journey is a testament to the strength and resilience she teaches in her books. As a child, she saw firsthand how hard—almost impossible — it was to rise above the unfortunate circumstances that were part of her everyday life. She vividly recalls struggling with a lack of resources in her community. Yet she participated in everything her public school had to offer, which instilled in her a deep desire to serve others.

A community leader for over three decades, Katherine has garnered recognition for her dedication to making a positive impact. Her journey includes founding Learn CPR America, LLC, and the Dr. Katherine Y. Brown (KYB) Leadership Academy. She has trained over 300,000 people in CPR for free and has mentored over 250 leaders through KYB. Her training initiatives have enabled her to host KYB conferences in Costa Rica, Colombia, South America, Dubai, South Africa, and the Turks and Caicos Islands.

Some of her leadership and civic engagement includes the Junior League; Jack and Jill of America, Inc. (Nashville Chapter Vice President, 2022–2024); The Links, Inc.; Top Ladies of Distinction, Inc.; Charms, Inc.; and Iota Phi Lambda Sorority, Inc. (Southern Region Outstanding Business Woman of the Year, 2023). She is also a member of the National Coalition of 100 Black Women.

She has served as Parenting and Family Chair and as a faculty member for the Maxwell Leadership Certified Team. She has traveled internationally, teaching as a coach with the John Maxwell Leadership Foundation, visiting locations such as Papua New Guinea, Panama, and the Dominican Republic. Her involvement further underscores her dedication to nurturing and guiding the next generation of leaders.

Katherine now enjoys life in Nashville, Tennessee, with her husband, four children, and two rescue dogs she affectionately refers to as her "furbabies."

DR. TSITSI HUNGWE

 Dr. Tsitsi Hungwe is a Zimbabwean-American, sought-after keynote speaker, writer, corporate trainer, and early professional career transition coach. Leveraging several years of experience in the dental industry, she helps early professional women confidently prepare for their next career chapter, whether starting, advancing, or transitioning into new careers. In line with her unyielding passion for helping others succeed, Dr. Tsitsi serves as founder and chief executive of Higher Mountaintops, LLC. She empowers students and professionals at corporations, universities, and organizations worldwide with her message of mastering mental resilience and mindset for successful transitions.

She has delivered inspiring live and virtual keynotes and leadership training for prominent organizations, including the Leadership Experience Tour, University of Michigan Women in Leadership Conference, Support DDS, and Leadership Hendricks County, among others. Dr. Tsitsi is a visionary recognized for her leadership, commitment, and contributions to her community and the next generation. She also serves as an independent certified leadership speaker, trainer, coach, and DISC Behavioral Analysis Consultant with the Maxwell Leadership Team.

She extends her heartfelt gratitude to Angela Hooper -Menifield, the visionary behind this anthology. In her words: "Angela has been a blessing in my life. I am grateful to and for her unwavering support, both personally and professionally, and her unconditional love for me. Our conversations inspired me to write my chapter, "Decision-Making Under Pressure: Thriving in Uncertainty.""

AMBER R. LETBETTER

Amber R. Letbetter is a dynamic, purpose-driven leader from Memphis, Tennessee, known for her unwavering commitment to advancing equity, empathy, and intentional leadership in the workplace. A proud millennial professional, Amber brings both lived experience and strategic insight to her work, helping organizations reimagine how they attract, engage, and retain diverse talent.

A graduate of the University of Missouri, Amber earned her Bachelor of Arts in American History in 2018. Since then, she has built a multifaceted career in human resources, talent acquisition, and diversity strategy, currently serving as Project Manager, Human Resources at Hertz Corporation. In this role, she leads cross-functional initiatives that blend people strategy with project execution to support a more inclusive and effective workforce. Her previous roles include Branding Talent Acquisition Partner, Regional Talent Acquisition Partner, and Talent Acquisition Supervisor, where she managed large-scale hiring initiatives, recruitment campaigns, and inclusion-driven talent strategies.

Amber is also an accomplished trainer and speaker, having presented at the Social Equity Leadership Conference in both 2019 and 2023, and at the National Conference of Minority Public Administrators, where she shared her insights on representation, access, and belong-

227

ing. She is passionate about bridging differences through meaningful dialogue and decision-making—a theme she powerfully explores in her *Leadership Unveiled* chapter, "Leading Across Differences: Equity, Empathy, and Everyday Choices."

Whether leading teams, launching initiatives, or advocating for underrepresented communities, Amber leads with heart, courage, and a strong belief that everyday choices have the power to transform leadership and culture.

SHARON EASON, CPA

 Sharon Eason, CPA, is an accomplished financial strategist, leadership advisor, and founder of Chase Eason & Associates, Inc., a boutique firm dedicated to helping small business owners achieve long-term sustainability through strategic tax planning, CFO services, and financial clarity. With over two decades of experience in tax planning, CFO services, audits, and business coaching, Sharon brings a rare mix of technical expertise and heart-centered guidance to the leaders she serves. She is widely recognized for her ability to translate complex financial matters into clear, actionable insights that drive results.

In her chapter, *"From Boss to Visionary: Transform Your Management Style into Real Leadership,"* Sharon offers a compelling framework for leaders ready to evolve beyond operational oversight and embrace purpose-driven leadership. Drawing from her transformation and years of advising both for-profit and nonprofit organizations, she provides a roadmap to build empowered teams, achieve strategic alignment, and cultivate legacy-minded growth.

Sharon is a Certified Maxwell Leadership Business Strategy Coach, a licensed CPA, and a Chartered Global Management Accountant in New York. She is also a member of the AICPA, the National Association of Tax Professionals, and the American Society of Tax Problem

Solvers. Her leadership is grounded in integrity, foresight, and an unwavering commitment to her clients' success.

She has served on the boards of two nonprofit foundations and remains active in her community. Beyond the boardroom, Sharon finds joy in reading, hiking, traveling, and exploring global cuisine, guided daily by faith, family, and the principle of Psalm 32:8.

DR. OLIVE L. CYRUS
DNP, MSA, BSN, RN-BC

Dr. Olive L. Cyrus is an energetic, initiative-taking, and collaborative nurse leader with thirty-six years of successful nursing practice. Her extensive experience includes service as a U.S. Air Force Active Duty Officer, serving as a surgical nurse and flight nurse, as well as leadership roles in the Department of Defense as Director of Quality Management and in the Veterans Administration as Chief Nurse for the Care Coordinator Program.

Dr. Olive recently retired after 27 years of federal service. She currently serves as the Quality Management Member Incident Unit Director with Trillium Health Resources MCO. Her background is rich in performance improvement, utilization management, and risk management.

Deeply connected to her community, Dr. Olive is actively involved with Meals on Wheels and the Congregational Nursing Program of Alamance County. She is a dedicated member of Elon First Baptist Church, where she serves as an usher, co-chair of the health ministry, and a Women's Ministry Council member. She is also a proud member of Alpha Kappa Alpha Sorority, Inc. Her hobbies include gardening, Zumba, walking, and connecting with people.

Dr. Olive is part of the Financial Literacy Campaign,

which aims to educate 30 million families by 2030. She is licensed in 11 states and is a Certified John Maxwell Life and Health Coach. She is also the CEO of OLC Consulting LLC, a company created to transform communities worldwide by equipping and empowering women with holistic success principles that integrate mind, body, and spirit, fostering personal growth and empowerment.

Education:
- **Doctor of Nursing Practice, 2012** Duke University, Durham, NC
- **Master of Science in Administration, 1995** Central Michigan University (Extended Program), Fayetteville, NC
- **Bachelor of Science in Nursing, 1989** Hampton University, Hampton, VA

Angela Jackson-Andrews

Angela Jackson-Andrews is an executive leadership strategist, certified life coach, and founder of Spirit of Excellence Coaching & Consulting. She is a transformational speaker with over 30 years of corporate and talent development experience, specializing in developing high-impact leaders.

She is a Certified Maxwell Leadership Speaker, coach, and trainer; a credentialed member of the International Coaching Federation (ICF); and holds certifications in DISC, Caliper, and Real Colors behavioral assessments. Angela is also a certified Life Purpose Coach and Life Success Coach, serving both national and international clients. Additionally, she is a Registered Corporate Training Executive through the LaFleur Leadership Institute.

Angela is a graduate of Mercer University in Macon, GA, with a BBA in Business Administration and a minor in Psychology. She is a contributing author of the anthology *Leadership Unveiled.*

Angela's mission is to build powerful women, influential leaders, and transformative organizations through tools that elevate voice, visibility, and value.

DR. SHANITA NOLAN

 Dr. ShaNita Nolan is an accomplished leadership development expert, learning and development practitioner, training program designer and instructor, workshop presenter, author, speaker, advocate, and coach with over two decades of experience in professional growth, leadership development, and personal development. She holds numerous professional certifications, including a Mental Health Coach certification from the American Association of Christian Counselors.

Her deep commitment to maternal and mental health advocacy extends to her involvement with the March of Dimes, the National Alliance on Mental Illness, and Mental Health America. Dr. Nolan serves on the Yet-Stand Inc. Board of Directors and the Federally Employed Women National Board of Directors.

Through her books, workshops, and speeches, she shares expertise on leadership, life, and navigating the complexities of mental and maternal health, while advocating for comprehensive support systems and inclusive policies. She founded Circle of Trust Leadership, Gathering the Fragments Ministry, and L3 Unlimited: platforms that empower personal, professional, leadership, and spiritual growth. These initiatives support women in healing, encourage them to share their stories, and promote holistic well-being, self-love, self-care, and resiliency.

Dr. Nolan is a mentor and champion for diverse groups, including young girls, single mothers, and survivors of sexual assault and domestic violence. Additionally, she hosts The Widows Lounge podcast, which is tailored to Christian widows and offers faith-based guidance and support through stories of resilience and hope.

References

Chapter 1: Dr. Cheryl Burton

1. Allen, J. (1903). *As a man thinketh.* New York, NY: Thomas Y. Crowell & Co.
2. Dyer, W. W. (2001). *There's a spiritual solution to every problem. HarperCollins.*
3. Walsch, N. D. (1998). *Conversations with God: An uncommon dialogue (Book 3). Putnam Publishing Group.*

Chapter 2: Leslie Britt

1. The Bible. (n.d.). The Passion Translation (TPT). Proverbs 4:1–2.
2. The Bible. (n.d.). *New International Version.* Proverbs 22:6; Romans 12:10; Colossians 3:23; Matthew 7:13.
3. Peterson, E. H. (2002). The Message: The Bible in Contemporary Language. NavPress.
4. Unknown. (n.d.). Integrity is doing the right thing, even when no one is watching [Quote]. Commonly attributed to C. S. Lewis.
5. Malcolm X. (n.d.). Education is the passport to the future, for tomorrow belongs to those who prepare for it today [Quote].
6. Maxwell, J. C. (n.d.). Leadership is influence, nothing more, nothing less [Quote].

Chapter 3: Dr. Robin K. Butler

1. Bradberry, T., & Greaves, J. (2009). *Emotional Intelligence 2.0. TalentSmart.*
2. Goleman, D. (1995). *Emotional intelligence: Why it can matter more than IQ. Bantam Books.*

3. Goleman, D. (2006). *Social intelligence: The new science of human relationships. Bantam Books.*
4. Travis, B., & Jean, G. (2010). *The Emotional Intelligence Quick Book: Everything You Need to Know to Put Your EQ to Work. Simon & Schuster.*
5. Goleman, D. (2005). *Emotional intelligence: Why it can matter more than IQ. Bantam.*
6. Goleman, D. (2019). *The emotionally intelligent leader. Harvard Business Press.*
7. Perez, J. (2014). Focus: The Hidden Driver of Excellence [review]/Goleman, Daniel. Journal of Applied Christian Leadership, 8(2), 103-105.

Chapter 4: Kenric Lynn

1. Acton, J. E. E. D. (1887, April 5). Letter to Bishop Mandell Creighton.
2. Brehm, J. W. (1966). *A Theory of Psychological Reactance. Academic Press.*
3. Casciaro, T., & Sousa Lobo, M. (2005). "Competent Jerks, Lovable Fools, and the Formation of Social Networks." *Harvard Business Review.*
4. Cialdini, R. B. (1984, 2001). *Influence: The Psychology of Persuasion. Harper Business.*
5. Covey, S. M. R. (2006). *The Speed of Trust. Free Press.*
6. French, J. R. P., & Raven, B. (1959). *"The Bases of Social Power." In D. Cartwright (Ed.), Studies in Social Power.* University of Michigan
7. Gallup. (2017). *State of the American Workplace.*
8. Hannah, S. T., Avolio, B. J., & Walumbwa, F. O. (2011). "Relationships Between Authentic Leader-

ship, Moral Courage, and Ethical and Pro-Social Behaviors." *Business Ethics Quarterly,* 21(4), 555–578.

9. Hill, L. A. (2003). *Becoming a Manager: How New Managers Master the Challenges of Leadership.* Harvard Business Review Press.

10. Judge, T. A., et al. (2004). "Transformational and Transactional Leadership: A Meta-Analytic Test of Their Relative Validity." *Journal of Applied Psychology, 89(5), 755–768.*

11. Keltner, D. (2016). *The Power Paradox: How We Gain and Lose Influence.* Penguin Press.

12. Kouzes, J. M., & Posner, B. Z. (2017). *The Leadership Challenge.* Wiley.

13. Lipman-Blumen, J. (2005). *The Allure of Toxic Leaders.* Oxford University Press.

14. McClelland, D. C. (1975). Power: *The Inner Experience.* Irvington Publishers.

15. Weber, M. (1947). *The Theory of Social and Economic Organization.* Free Press.

16. Zimbardo, P. G. (1971). "The Power and Pathology of Imprisonment." *Congressional Record.*

Chapter 5: Dr. Katherine Y. Baines Brown

1. Blanchard, K., & Hodges, P. (2005). *Lead like Jesus: Lessons from the greatest leadership role model of all time.* Thomas Nelson.

2. Brown, B. (2018). *Dare to lead: Brave work. Tough conversations. Whole hearts.* Random House.

3. Covey, S. R. (2004). *The 7 habits of highly effective people: Powerful lessons in personal change.* Free Press. (Original work published 1989)

4. Kouzes, J. M., & Posner, B. Z. (2017). *The leadership challenge: How to make extraordinary things happen in organizations (6th ed.).* Jossey-Bass.
5. Maxwell, J. C. (1993). *Developing the leader within you.* Thomas Nelson.
6. Maxwell, J. C. (2005). *The 360° leader: Developing your influence from anywhere in the organization.* Thomas Nelson.

Chapter 6: Angela Hooper-Menifield
1. Deloitte. (2023). *2023 Global human capital trends: New fundamentals for a boundaryless world.* Deloitte Insights.
2. https://www2.deloitte.com/insights/us/en/focus/human-capital-trends.html
3. Gallup. (2015). *State of the American manager: Analytics and advice for leaders.* Gallup Press.
4. *https://www.gallup.com/services/182138/state-american-manager-report.aspx*
5. Google re: Work. (n.d.). *Project Oxygen: Why Google's managers matter. https:// rework.withgoogle.com/print/guides/managers-project-oxygen/*
6. McKinsey & Company. (2022). *The state of organizations: 2022 report.*
7. *https://www.mckinsey.com/capabilities/people-and-organizational-performance/our-insights/the-state-of-organizations-2022*

Chapter 7: Angela Hooper-Menifield

1. Edison, T. (n.d.). Vision without execution is just hallucination [Quote]. Retrieved from https://www.goodreads.com/quotes/558445-vision-without-execution-is-just-hallucination
2. Sinek, S. (2009). *Start with why: How great leaders inspire everyone to take action.* Portfolio.
3. Schultz, H., & Gordon, J. (2011). *Onward: How Starbucks fought for its life without losing its soul.* Rodale Books.

Chapter 9: Angela Hooper Menifield

1. Gallup. (2023). *State of the Global Workplace: 2023 Report.* Gallup, Inc.
2. https://www.gallup.com/workplace/349484/state-of-the-global-workplace.aspx

Chapter 10: Amber Reneé Letbetter

1. Gallup. (2023). *State of the Global Workplace: 2023 Report.* Gallup, Inc.
2. *https://www.gallup.com/workplace/349484/state-of-the-global-workplace.aspx*
3. Derald Wing Sue, Capodilupo, C. M., Torino, G. C., Bucceri, J. M., Holder, A. M. B., Nadal, K. L., & Esquilin, M. (2007). Racial microaggressions in everyday life: Implications for clinical practice. *American Psychologist, 62(4), 271–286. https://doi.org/10.1037/0003-066X.62.4.271*
4. Edmonson, A. C. (1999). Psychological safety and learning behavior in work teams. *Administrative Sci-*

ence Quarterly, 44(2), 350–383. https://doi.org/10.2307/2666999

5. Gonzalez, J. (2019). *Culture and Equity in the Workplace: A Practical Guide to Inclusive Leadership. Equity Press.*
6. Bourke, J., & Espedido, A. (2020). Why inclusive leaders are good for organizations, and how to become one. *Harvard Business Review. https://hbr.org/2020/03/why-inclusive-leaders-are-good-for-organizations-and-how-to-become-one*

Chapter 11: Sharon Eason

1. Brown, B. (2018). *Dare to lead: Brave work. Tough conversations. Whole hearts.* Random House.
2. Maxwell, J. C. (2011). *The 5 levels of leadership: Proven steps to maximize your potential.* Center Street.
3. McKeown, G. (2014). *Essentialism: The disciplined pursuit of less.* Crown Business.
4. Pink, D. H. (2009). *Drive: The surprising truth about what motivates us.* Riverhead Books.
5. Scott, K. (2017). *Radical candor: Be a kick-ass boss without losing your humanity.* St. Martin's Press.
6. Sinek, S. (2014). *Leaders eat last: Why some teams pull together and others don't.* Portfolio/Penguin.

Chapter 12: Dr. Katherine Y. Baines Brown

1. Brown, B. (2018). *Dare to lead: Brave work. Tough conversations. Whole hearts.* Random House.
2. Patterson, K., Grenny, J., McMillan, R., & Switzler, A. (2012). *Crucial conversations: Tools for talking*

when stakes are high (2nd ed.). McGraw-Hill Education.

3. Heifetz, R., Grashow, A., & Linsky, M. (2009). *The practice of adaptive leadership: Tools and tactics for changing your organization and the world.* Harvard Business Press.

4. Goleman, D. (2006). *Emotional intelligence: Why it can matter more than IQ.* Bantam.

5. Scott, K. (2017). *Radical candor: Be a kick-ass boss without losing your humanity.* St. Martin's Press.

Chapter 13: Olive Cyrus

1. Bradberry, T., & Greaves, J. (2009). *Emotional Intelligence 2.0. TalentSmart.*

2. Goleman, D. (2006). *Emotional intelligence: Why it can matter more than IQ.* Bantam Books.

3. Harvard Business Review. (2023, May 18). *Why middle managers are so burned out. Harvard Business Publishing.https://hbr.org/2023/05/why-middle-managers-are-so-burned-out*

4. Maxwell, J. C. (2007). *The 21 Irrefutable Laws of Leadership: Follow them and people will follow you (10th Anniversary ed.).* Thomas Nelson.

5. Maxwell, J. C. (2012). *The 15 invaluable laws of growth: Live them and reach your potential.* Center Street.

6. Maxwell, J. C. (2001). *Developing the leader within you 2.0. HarperCollins Leadership.*

7. Myers & Briggs Foundation. (n.d.). *MBTI basics. https://www.myersbriggs.org/my-mbti-personality-type/mbti-basics/*

8. Pearman, R. R. (2002). *Hardwired leadership: Unleashing the power of personality to become a new millennium leader.* Davies-Black Publishing.
9. The DISC Personality Testing Company. (n.d.). *What is DISC? https://www.discprofile.com/what-is-disc*
10. Van Velsor, E., McCauley, C. D., & Ruderman, M. N. (2010). *The Center for Creative Leadership handbook of leadership development (3rd ed.).* Jossey-Bass.

Chapter 14: Angela Jackson-Andrews

1. Harvard Business Review. (2020, March 5). *Why sponsorship is key to diversity and inclusion. https://hbr.org/2020/03/why-sponsorship-is-key-to-diversity-and-inclusion*
2. LinkedIn. (2023). *The ultimate list of hiring statistics for 2023. https://business.linkedin.com/talent-solutions/blog/trends-and-research/2023/the-ultimate-list-of-hiring-statistics*
3. McKinsey & Company. (2023). *Women in the workplace 2023. https://www.mckinsey.com/featured-insights/diversity-and-inclusion/women-in-the-workplace*
4. The Holy Bible, New International Version. (1978). *Luke 12:48 ("To whom much is given, much is required").*

Chapter 15: Dr. ShaNita Nolan

1. Angelou, M. (n.d.). People will forget what you said, people will forget what you did, but people will never forget how you made them feel. Goodreads. https://

www.goodreads.com/quotes/18542

2. Bennis, W. (1989). *On becoming a leader.* Addison-Wesley.

3. Maxwell, J. C. (2015). *Intentional living: Choosing a life that matters.* Center Street.

4. Maxwell, J. C. (2007). *The 21 Irrefutable Laws of Leadership: Follow them and people will follow you (10th anniversary ed.).* Thomas Nelson.

NOTES